The Secrets of
Angel Healing

SABI HILMI

ABOUT THE AUTHOR

Sabi Hilmi always felt that there was more to life than she could see. Like everyone, she has been faced with challenges and disappointments, which have on occasion taken away her hope of finding and experiencing success in life and love. Her awakening to the divine energy of the Angels led her to begin the journey of healing her past and gave her back this hope. After many years of searching, Sabi eventually found her life's purpose: to teach about Angels and to channel their healing energy to help others find love and happiness too.

The Secrets of Angel Healing

How to Channel Your Guardian Angel and Find Happiness

SABI HILMI

MICHAEL JOSEPH
an imprint of
PENGUIN BOOKS

MICHAEL JOSEPH

Published by the Penguin Group

Penguin Books Ltd, 80 Strand, London WC2R ORL, England

Penguin Group (USA) Inc., 375 Hudson Street, New York, New York 10014, USA

Penguin Group (Canada), 90 Eglinton Avenue East, Suite 700, Toronto, Ontario, Canada M4P 2Y3
(a division of Pearson Penguin Canada Inc.)

Penguin Ireland, 25 St Stephen's Green, Dublin 2, Ireland (a division of Penguin Books Ltd)

Penguin Group (Australia), 250 Camberwell Road, Camberwell, Victoria 3124, Australia
(a division of Pearson Australia Group Pty Ltd)

Penguin Books India Pvt Ltd, 11 Community Centre, Panchsheel Park, New Delhi – 110 017, India

Penguin Group (NZ), 67 Apollo Drive, Rosedale, North Shore 0632, New Zealand
(a division of Pearson New Zealand Ltd)

Penguin Books (South Africa) (Pty) Ltd, 24 Sturdee Avenue, Rosebank,
Johannesburg 2196, South Africa

Penguin Books Ltd, Registered Offices: 80 Strand, London WC2R ORL, England

www.penguin.com

First published 2011

1

Copyright © Sabi Hilmi, 2011

The moral right of the author has been asserted

Set in 11.75/14pt Garamond MT Std
Typeset by Jouve (UK), Milton Keynes

Printed in Great Britain by Clays Ltd, St Ives plc

A CIP catalogue record for this book is available from the British Library

ISBN: 978-0-718-15701-2

www.greenpenguin.co.uk

Penguin Books is committed to a sustainable future
for our business, our readers and our planet.
The book in your hands is made from paper
certified by the Forest Stewardship Council.

Contents

Prologue: My Personal Journey   1

PART I

Introduction To Angels   11

PART II

Angel Healing   23

Chakras   31

Exercise: Feeling Angel Starlight Energy   26

Meditation   35

Meditation: Meeting Your Guardian Angel   41

PART III

Connecting and Communicating
with Angels   45

Intuition   47

Meditation: Connecting with the Angels   48

Channelling   50

Meditation: Communicating with the Angels   54

PART IV

Archangels — 57

Archangel Michael — 59

Archangel Raphael — 63

Archangel Chamuel — 66

Archangel Gabriel — 69

Meditation: Visiting the Archangels' Sanctuary — 71

PART V

Angel Healing for the Body — 75

Illness — 79

Weight Problems — 87

Attractiveness — 95

Lethargy — 101

Sleep and Astral Travel — 107

Depression — 116

Sensuality — 122

Practical Exercises with Archangel Raphael — 128

PART VI

Angel Healing for the Mind — 133

Positive Thinking — 137

Overcoming Fears — 143

Having a Successful Career — 149

Creativity 158

Confidence 165

Stress 172

Abundance 180

Practical Exercises with Archangel Gabriel 186

PART VII

Angel Healing for the Heart 191

Loneliness 197

Rejection 204

Bullying 211

Bereavement 218

Heartbreak 225

Forgiveness 233

Finding Love and Romance 240

Practical Exercises with Archangel Chamuel 247

PART VIII

Angel Healing for the Soul 253

Awaken Your Soul 257

Intuition 264

Cleansing 271

Negative Energy 277

Attracting Soul Mates 284

CONTENTS

Meeting Your Soul Family   291

Living as an Earth Angel   299

Practical Exercises with Archangel Michael   306

Acknowledgements   311

Prologue: My Personal Journey

Spiritual Awakening

As a child, I felt isolated because of my severe shyness, low self-esteem and lack of confidence. I found interacting with people very difficult, so I developed a very introverted personality and often felt invisible as well as worthless. The breaking point came in my early twenties, caused by the emotional heartbreak I had suffered over the years. Even though I was blessed to have the love of my family, it never filled the emptiness deep within my heart. I realize now that I spent many years searching for love from a significant other in order to fill that void and make me feel whole. This self-destructive behaviour led me towards my spiritual awakening. I had always been a lost soul, and my lack of confidence continued to affect all my relationships – friends, family, schoolfriends and colleagues. I couldn't allow people to come too far into my world, so my only option was to be on my own. I spent many years trying to figure out why I was living this way when I knew deep down that there was so much more to life. Luckily, I had one very special person who believed in me and my dreams, and she has given me hope throughout my life. My mother told me to keep my faith and aim high, and that nothing was impossible.

The year 2000 was my turning point. I was at my lowest ebb emotionally, and was mentally exhausted by trying to make sense of all the chaotic, negative thoughts in my mind. This had an adverse affect on my physical health, and that was the wake-up call to either give up or fight for survival. I turned to prayer, and no matter how difficult or bad the situation I was in, I always knew there was a powerful force that saw everything I was going through.

As a child, I drew great comfort from prayer. It was the only place I felt listened to and understood. I was given a set of holy prayer books by a close family member, and although I didn't fully understand what I was reading, I realized that each short, specific prayer was exerting a different, positive impact on me. Gradually, as I grew older, I started to feel a presence in the room with me, and at times this would really frighten me and I'd run down to my mother crying. Other times, I'd feel so serene and peaceful; it was like I was dreaming. I'd feel cleansed and purified by the divine energy I felt flowing through me. I created a little sacred space in my room where I would pray each night without fail.

Writing became an essential daily routine. I started jotting thoughts and feelings into my diaries, and things seemed to make more sense and fall into perspective. Writing helped me to clear my mind, and I found that my emotions were more under control. One of the first profound experiences I had was through creative automatic writing. At the time, I was searching for answers to some questions relating to a situation I was going through. On a normal day of scribbling down notes, something took over my mind and I no longer had any control over what I was writing. That was the beginning of a very special gift – channelling spiritual guidance from my spirit guides, or Angels. I wasn't quite sure where this information was coming from, but I knew it wasn't coming from me, as it was coming through on to the paper faster than my mind could function. My arm would ache at the end of it. I waited for a name to come through as a sign-off, but all I'd ever get was a big X.

I felt very excited about what was happening, but a little frustrated too, at times, when I tried to force information to come through and it wouldn't. At first, I wanted advice on how to deal with my present situation, and then slowly I started getting insights into my future. I would receive a loud, clear message in my mind when information was ready to come through to me, and it would come through so fast I couldn't recognize my own handwriting. This divine guidance was very comforting for me at such a challenging, negative phase in my life. I felt cursed, as if the world was against me. My only hope was that someone somewhere would hear my prayers and feel my pain, and send me the opportunity to change things.

One evening I was at a friend's house and I started explaining what was happening to me. This friend was a complete sceptic and told me to pull myself together and stay focused on reality. I did have another friend, however, who was more of a believer in the spiritual realm, and she asked me to try and do her a 'psychic reading'. I'd had a few readings myself by that time and had always been fascinated as to how it all worked. I closed my eyes and went into a deep relaxation mode where I couldn't open my eyes. I went on an internal journey and started seeing something that seemed to be the story of a little girl. I saw a garden and described what was happening and who was present in real detail. All I could hear was my friend's surprise at how I could possibly know this information. I had described an episode in her childhood that she clearly remembered, and also an aunt of hers who had passed away. I was shocked by this experience, and it took me a while to bring my consciousness back into the room. Both of my friends were surprised, but the sceptical one was scared at the effect doing the reading had had on me and told me not to do it again. It left me with many questions, and this is how I began my journey into spiritual development.

Spiritual Development

My quest for spiritual development initially came from an interest in healing myself. I found a Spiritual Development College in London, and by studying all the courses available, I began my learning journey, and things started to make more sense. It was good to know that there were many people who were experiencing similar feelings of guidance to those I was. During one of the meditation classes, we connected to our Guardian Angels, and it was the most serene experience I had ever had. It was like a reunion with a family after being separated for a very long time. It was very emotional and exciting, and I didn't want to come out of the serenity I had found. From then on, I'd spend hours channelling spiritual advice on how to change my life for the better, how to find the meaning and purpose of why I was here. I studied and became a Reiki master, which led me through a complete physical, mental, emotional and spiritual detoxification. This was not an easy process, as everything I had bottled up within me until then was coming up to the surface as I channelled new life-force energy into my body, mind, heart and soul to remove old, stale patterns. As I had activated my chakras (energy centres within the body), my channelling and intuitive skills developed immensely. I was linking into my spirit guides and Guardian Angel a lot more quickly to ask for help with certain situations for myself and others, which made me feel really supported, loved and safe.

Spiritual Healing

I became very sensitive, especially to the negative energy of others; I would pick up on their pain or emotions. I'd feel sick in my stomach and very stressed out when I was around people who had been arguing, and I'd feel very emotional around people who were experiencing problems in their life. It was a constant internal battle trying to avoid these situations and people. I felt that I needed protection from the 'evil eye', which only led me towards living a very fear-based life – thinking that the world was against me. When my energy levels were low, my luck was always bad and I was unhappy, especially in terms of relationships of any kind. I was fascinated by the concept that I had had past lives and that I had carried forward into this life some karma that needed resolving in order for my soul to learn and evolve. I was guided by my Guardian Angel and the Angel of Transmutation, Archangel Zadkiel, to burn and dissolve everything that was keeping my energies tied to the past.

As I became more sensitive and was able to see and feel subtle energies, depending on my inner thoughts and feelings, I would see, hear and feel the equivalent energy forms around me.

It took me a long time to understand how curses, or 'psychic attacks', worked, and how another human being could have the power to influence the happiness of others in a negative way. Angels taught me that everything is done through choice. Each person is entitled to have their own thoughts and emotions, and to perform any action as they wish. The Angels also told me that, with each choice, there would be a cause, and there would be a corresponding effect. This is based on the law of karma: for every action (cause), there is a reaction (effect), even if the effect presents itself at a much later date.

During the years I was aware of negative energy forms around me, I felt that my own energy was being attacked, and I was desperate to find a way to stop this happening and be free in every way. This was something I couldn't talk to many people about, as most would dismiss it, saying that there was no such thing. I did however have an idea of where this darkness was coming from and why it was being directed towards me. The distress this was causing me in my life was unbearable, and it was making me physically ill and extremely depressed. This lasted a long time, and meant I could only trust and have faith in my Guardian Angel. She reassured me constantly that my energy was being cleansed. She also told me that I had to forgive those I was holding up to blame if my life was to be purified. I found this difficult, as I felt so hurt by those who I believed were responsible for my unhappiness.

Through spiritual healing, I learned that forgiveness is not about condoning the action, but about learning to accept the present moment and take control of the future rather than dwelling on the past. My Guardian Angel helped me to understand that everything I had experienced so far was leading towards my spiritual awakening and clearing my negative karma. For at least five years, I was in and out of severe bouts of depression caused by this negative energy. Through dedication, trust and willpower, I finally came to believe that I had broken the spell with the power of love, Angels and spiritual healing. I began to feel like a new person, completely at peace. I felt strong, grounded and lighter than before. I knew that I had been set free and that all barriers, negative energies and attacks had been healed to enable me to start a fresh new life.

Angel Healing

My first Angel Healing experience happened when the closest person to me in my life, my beloved mother, was encountering some health problems related to her heart. One evening, feeling helpless by her side, I reached out to God through prayer and asked for help. I fell into a deep trance, my eyes closed, and I sensed a feeling of heaviness over my shoulders. I saw a bright light piercing through the darkness in my mind, and my hands were guided through a magnetic pull straight to my mother's heart. The swirling lights formed into a huge ball of energy which stood behind me, channelling the lights through my body, and through my hands into her heart. I was unable to open my eyes. Although this lasted only about ten minutes, we both felt as if we had spent hours in a different world.

The difficulties my mother had been facing before this healing experience were irregular heart palpitations which would leave her breathless, even after climbing just a few stairs. After the short channelling session, although she was still unable to open her eyes, her heartbeat changed incredibly quickly back to normal, and her breathing also returned to normal.

My shock and amazement at what had happened led me to find out more about energy healing. As I had always been interested in knowing what my future held, I had consulted a few psychic mediums in the past for readings, and been told that I had healing abilities which would become apparent later in my life. I never knew what this meant and so wasn't interested in pursuing it. I had so many questions about life: What was the meaning of it all? Why was I here? Why do I feel so alone, even with people around me? Before my spiritual healing journey began, I was unfulfilled, empty and suffered from depression. My hopes for happiness and love were very low. Keeping my trust and faith, however, I felt blessed to have been given the ability to intuitively see, hear and feel the Heavenly Angels who guided me to change my life for the better.

Life Transformation

My life began to change dramatically. Although I spent many hours doing ordinary work, inwardly I was yearning to do something more fulfilling. By changing my thought patterns and beliefs, an opportunity arose when I was offered redundancy and a lump sum towards any form of study. This gave me financial security, and I went on to buy my 'Angel Sanctuary'. Through meditations, reading books, studying and lifestyle changes, I was feeling physically and emotionally happier. I began to communicate with my Guardian Angel verbally and would receive answers through the feelings she communicated to me. A 'yes' would be a very happy warm sensation in my heart; 'no' would be a sad sensation. I also learned to use a pendulum, which would turn in different ways for yes and no.

The most effective method of communicating with my Guardian Angel was through creative writing. Unfortunately, this would only happen occasionally, but when it did, very in-depth answers were given back. I've kept yearly diaries filled with channelled information from many years ago, regarding all areas of my life, and will share extracts from them in this book. The world of Angels existed within me, and although I developed to see, hear and feel them very clearly, it took me a long time to share this gift with others. As my life changed for the better, I began gently to deliver messages of healing and inspiration to others.

Very soon afterwards, I was asked by my spiritual development teacher to teach about Angel Healing at the college and, from there, I continued to go on and help people with some form of Angel guidance or healing. I became a qualified practitioner in Angel Healing and went on to set up purely-angels. com. I regularly teach people how they can invite the Angels and

Archangels into their lives for guidance, healing and empowerment towards achieving and maintaining happiness, love and well-being. By writing *The Secrets of Angel Healing*, I have been on another empowering personal transformation and feel privileged to share the Angels' love with the world.

A Message About This Book

June 2006

Darling Sabi,

In divine timing, you are to write a book based on your experiences of love. We ask that you practise being a clear divine channel of love and light at all times. Remember: love heals everything in your world. You have been blessed to experience a deep soul connection with another, who has played an enormous role in your life. Learn to trust the divine process, my dear child, and stop hurrying. You will continue having these soul connections with mates in your soul family; the next one is on the way to you physically, so be prepared! You will be blessed to receive the answers to your many questions through this connection, and this soul will play a huge role in helping you to write your book.

If you think that you have already experienced love in its greatest form, you are mistaken. Remember that you get back from the universe what you give to others. Learn to love, cherish and honour yourself fully and unconditionally.

We now reveal to you your life purpose: you are to teach about the Angels' love, which is available to everyone, and how to live the Heaven on Earth experience, as you yourself have achieved through your tribulations. When you are fully ready, we Angels will channel the contents of your book through you. You must do all that you can to live life from an Angels' perspective if you wish this book to be written. Raise your energy by meditating and looking after yourself physically, mentally, emotionally and spiritually. Anxiety, worry or fear will only hold you back and delay the process of you achieving your mission, which has been set by above.

We love you always, always with you, X

PART I:

INTRODUCTION TO ANGELS

The Secrets of Angel Healing has been channelled to bring the reader a different perspective on how to deal with everyday, real-life situations using the gift available to us all of Angel Healing. The book will take you, the reader, on a journey of development, from meeting your own Guardian Angel, to healing your body, mind, heart and soul through Angel Healing, to becoming a natural intuitor and the creator of your own happiness.

First, I will introduce the Angels, then describe their purpose and how they can help. I will also discuss healing and teach you many techniques which will develop your intuition skills and lead you towards all-round well-being. In the sections on healing your body, mind, heart and soul I will provide examples of the main challenges people are faced with in today's world, and show how the Angels can help. They will provide you with a completely new perspective on what may seem like a major problem. Any difficulty you may be experiencing will be transmuted by their loving, healing and powerful energy – love. When you understand this, your life will become fulfilled and balanced, and you will become full of optimism and enthusiasm to use your abilities to create the life you wish to have and to achieve your goals. But most of all, you will learn to love yourself and your life experience on Earth.

Once your healing journey has been completed, you will have all the techniques and wisdom to live your life, and see everything from a brand-new perspective, believing that love is the biggest power in your life and that negativity is the lack of love. You will be able to empathize with those still on their healing journey without judging them, instead lovingly supporting and assisting them with your newly found knowledge and purified energy.

This book is designed not only for people who are already on a healing journey but also for those who may be curious about the Angels and how they can assist in healing your body, mind, heart and soul. It contains practical advice as well as more sacred methods, such as meditations, and mind-reprogramming techniques, such as affirmations. The Angel Healing Technique and Secrets will transform you on more levels than you can imagine and will bring miracles into your life. You will begin to notice confirmation that your Angels are around you and that they are hearing your calls. Your Guardian Angel has been waiting to connect with you for a very long time, as it is their greatest pleasure to guide you to experience love and happiness.

Each section of Angel Healing for the body, mind, heart and soul contains seven challenging situations with channelled guidance from the Angels on how to heal them. There is a healing meditation for each one, along with a practical exercise to enhance the healing on a physical level. As you apply the secrets and invoke the assistance of the angelic beings, you will begin to notice miraculous outcomes, way beyond your rationale or expectations. The results are enhanced with your personal dedication to change and your determination to follow the process through. The Secrets aim to release the negativity that surrounds your situation from your past, to change the way it is negatively affecting you in the present and to empower you to create your desired future.

*

The Secrets of Angel Healing can be used to develop the way you live your life physically, the way you choose your thoughts mentally, the way you feel emotionally, and the way you believe in yourself spiritually. The following are some of the benefits you can expect to achieve when you find happiness with the help of your Guardian Angel:

∞ Physically: You will feel a lot more energetic and enthusiastic about living your life when you take the focus away from your difficulties. You will feel less discouraged and fatigued each day as you look forward to creating your desires. When you are happier, you will feel physically stronger and fitter in every way, improving the flow of life-force energy within you and boosting your immune system.

∞ Mentally: By eliminating your negative thoughts, you will feel a lot more positive and alert and become aware of your thinking patterns. The beneficial instructions from the Angels will become deeply embedded into your subconscious mind, as when you are relaxed, you are at your most susceptible and receptive to new ideas. These new, positive suggestions will cause a deep and lasting impression on your happiness when you take control of your mental activity and gain clarity.

∞ Emotionally: Your nerves will become calmer and steadier, bringing you feelings of serenity. Happiness generates emotions of contentment and an overwhelming feeling of love for your life. This will lead you naturally to attract more love, friends and relationships into your life. Happiness is a very contagious and influential state of being, and being happy will make you a very popular and attractive person.

∞ Spiritually: You will feel contentment and peace, knowing that you are fulfilled in your life, as you continue living a purposeful and meaningful life. Happiness promotes confidence, and confidence demotes the fears that have been holding you back for so long. The feelings of happiness lift your spirit higher and higher, and when you are in sync with the laws of the universe, manifesting your desires become effortless.

About Angels

The definition of 'Angel' is 'messenger'. Angels are celestial beings which have been created from the energy of unconditional love and act as messengers between Heaven and Earth. The Angels are androgynous beings of light, but at the same time they possess both feminine and masculine qualities. There are many different types of Angels, and each one has a position in the angelic hierarchy. Each has a different role to play, responsibilities and special qualities to bring into our lives. Ultimately, the Angels' goal is to open our hearts to love, awaken our consciousness with wisdom, to enable us to think positively without limitations and to live the happiest life possible by achieving all our desires.

The Angels *want* to help you:

> We ask that you call upon us Angels, as we thoroughly enjoy our responsibility of service. We wish to serve our creator by channelling unconditional love, guidance and healing to all souls. You do not have to believe in us until you are satisfied of our existence. We will always believe in you. We will lovingly teach you how to spread love and light through your world, to make it a better place.

Many Angels are connecting with Earth now in order to help

us with the challenging times we face and the transitional phase the planet is going through due to the evolution of humanity's consciousness. Although the Angels wish to help us all the time, in every single situation, due to the law of free will the Angels are limited in what they can do without being called upon by humans. Each person has a responsibility to choose their emotions, thoughts and actions, therefore the Angels cannot intervene even if they know that what the person is choosing does not serve their highest good.

Angels do not judge anyone's decisions or behaviour; they will always lovingly respond to your calls when you are ready to make a change. They know that your life is all about learning through experience and resolving karmic situations brought forward from previous lifetimes in order to continue your journey towards spiritual evolution. View the Angels as your little helpers, as those you can trust to provide support, those who genuinely care about your well-being. Angels patiently await your calls for their involvement so that they can lift the burdens of your everyday, stressful responsibilities. They wish for you to be free and enjoy your experiences in the human body and in your beautiful world.

Angels can help in many ways; they can bring you healing, inspiration and guidance in solving problems. They are like loyal friends who will never let you down and will rejoice in your success and happiness. Once you invite the Angels into your life, you will notice major transformations and positive shifts beginning to take place. Your healing journey begins with trust and by raising your awareness in order to perceive the Angels' messages. Always invoke the Angels for the highest and best good for everyone involved, ethically and with gratitude for their help. Accepting their love and healing energy will guide you towards fulfilment and contentment in all areas of your life. Everyone has inherent intuition skills which are waiting to be awakened and developed. These are blocked by fear, doubts and negative energy. Once these are removed through Angel Healing, you will listen naturally to your intuition as well as to the Angels on how you can better your life and achieve all your desires.

Angels live in a place called the angelic realm. They do not have physical form but existence on an energy frequency much higher than that of the physical matter of our world. As the energy frequencies of humanity and Earth start to shift through Angel Healing, it becomes easier to make a connection with the angelic realm. Angels who are called upon for help float between the two realms, acting as divine messengers and responding to our calls for healing, guidance, assistance and unconditional love.

There are many types of Angels, with specific purposes, and belonging to different groups.

Archangels

Archangels are Angels which have evolved through service. They watch over the groups of Angels, Guardian Angels and humanity. These powerful beings of light have their own purposes to fulfil, and they respond to our calls instantly. All Angels are able to transcend time and space in order to help bring healing to our lives, however the Archangels are the most powerful in what they can achieve. No matter how difficult your situation may be, they are able to perform miraculous healing for your highest good. Archangels are extremely intelligent and wise. They carry the divine knowledge and will provide answers to difficult situations your mind has thought impossible. I will talk more about Archangels in a later chapter.

Guardian Angels

Each person is born with a Guardian Angel which stays with them throughout all lives. Your Guardian Angel knows absolutely everything about you, things that even you may not know. They recall what you have experienced in previous lifetimes, as a child, and they know what your next lifetime will entail. You can find all this out by communicating with your personal Angel. They are dedicated to you alone. They will, however, lovingly help your loved ones too. Your Angel loves you unconditionally no matter what mistakes you may have made, and will never judge you. Throughout your life, other Angels will step in to work with your Guardian Angel, especially when you are going through major life transitions.

Guardian Angels never reincarnate into physical form, therefore they see everything through the eyes of purity and unconditional love. Like Archangels, they are very intelligent and wise beings who know what is best for us, however they will never impose their wisdom upon the person they are guiding. Nothing is impossible for them to achieve, and their wish is for us humans to have faith, as they do.

Guardian Angels have much compassion for humanity and all the challenges we face in our life on Earth. Your Guardian Angel wants to help you to find and maintain inner peace and to keep you away from negative influences. Once you have found this inner peace, you are shown the truth of your life purpose. Each person has a special gift to bring to the world, either through their talents or through their wisdom. Guardian Angels help us along the path to success in our aims, removing the limitations we place on ourselves.

You have a Guardian Angel who is always with you and whose purpose is to guide you throughout your life. This Angel has many responsibilities, but there are also rules: Angels cannot intervene in your life or in your decisions unless you want them to. They will be with you always during your soul's journey, whether or Earth or in different realms. Your Guardian Angel is dedicated to you and will protect you, especially in emergencies, until it's your time to move on to a different realm, when it is their responsibility to help you through the transition.

Your Guardian Angel is very aware of your mission and purpose in this life, even if you are unaware or have lost sight of it. Before you were incarnated, your life path was chosen by your soul with the help of your Guardian Angel and spiritual guides, but in coming into the physical body, each of us becomes influenced by the group consciousness of the world we live in. Your Guardian Angel patiently waits for you to reawaken and remember them. Even though you have a higher purpose to follow in your life, your soul needs experience before it can reach the point where it wants and is able to accept change. Your Guardian Angel can only support you through these painful experiences by giving you the knowledge that something very good will come out of a negative situation. They are able to see the end result and the future, so they secretly pour the energy of love and patience into your heart.

Your Guardian Angel is mostly able to connect with you while you are asleep. This is because your conscious mind is then still and silent, free from the mind's chatter. While you sleep, your Guardian Angel will talk to you about your situation and will give you an insight into the outcome. At the same time, you both meet with your spirit guides, who will remind you of your next step along your particular path.

Your Guardian Angel will send healing energy through you, so that you will wake up feeling refreshed and ready to face the world, knowing that you are fully charged and revitalized.

Throughout your day you may have recollections, a sense of déjà vu, of what you discussed with your Guardian Angel while you were asleep. Your Guardian Angel is allowed to send you healing energy and love without your permission, but it is up to you to consciously accept this and bring change into your life. Your Guardian Angel will appear to you in the form that you are most likely to recognize them, whatever resonates most with your own energy. If you adore children and you are young at heart, your Guardian Angel may appear as a small cherub! However, if you are an executive manager of a law firm, your Guardian Angel may choose to appear as a figure of authority. With regard to your Guardian Angel's name, during meditation, or through your intuition, you will be given a name that represents their energy. Guardian Angels do not actually have names; the names are given only for our benefit, so we can identify them. If you are unable to hear their name, your Guardian Angel is happy for you to choose a name that feels right to you.

My Guardian Angel is called Exeline. During a very beautiful meditation, I was shown that she is golden and very large, compared to my spirit guide, Ptara, who is physically very similar to me. Angel Exeline was the one who channelled written messages through me for many years before I actually connected with her spiritually. She is a lovely light being who guided me through all the challenges I have faced in my life, right up until the point where I was ready to teach Angel Healing to others, and she is still with me.

She has been telling me for many years that an opportunity to write this book would come about. About four years ago I was guided to buy a very unique blank notebook which I somehow could never pick up to use, as I always had a feeling I wasn't ready. I had placed it in my cupboard, where I would see it every day, not knowing what I would ever write in it. In 2009, I was told loud and clear to pick it up and start writing. This message came straight after I had finished creating my website. I was told to write about my purpose and intention in building it. The information just flowed through naturally. I was then asked to write about every single fear I had within me that was blocking me from achieving my purpose and intention. As soon as I wrote about all my fears and dealt with them internally, it seemed as if the opportunity to write a book about Angels came about by chance. But I knew that this was the Angel's work behind the scenes, and I heard Exeline saying, 'As promised, you are now ready to write a book about your experiences. Every part of your journey has been relevant to this book, it has all been so that you will be able to teach about Angel Healing. Much love and Angel blessings!'

Earth Angels

Angels never become human, however each person does have an angelic self within them. This may also be known as the soul. When this angelic self is awakened, your connection to the angelic realm will be very strong and, consequently, you will be living as an Angel on Earth. Your personality will have the same qualities as those found within Angels, such as innocence, unconditional love and purity. The soul knows what it feels like to love unconditionally, as the Angels do in Heaven. Being soul-conscious means living, acting, knowing, teaching and loving as an actual Angel. This may seem challenging and even impossible to imagine at this moment, however, after completing the programme of Angel Healing for the body, mind, heart and soul in this book, you will have a completely different perspective on life. You will be able to see yourself, others and life through the eyes of an Angel. The essential part of this healing journey is to be able to love others like an Angel. The more you awaken and project pure qualities, the quicker your healing journey progresses and, eventually, your whole being will integrate with the Angels. The benefits of this are phenomenal: living a Heavenly life on Earth is a wonderful experience.

PART II:

ANGEL HEALING

Angel Healing is a technique whereby angelic beings and their healing energies are invoked for the benefit of healing. The Angels provide their energy of love, wisdom and guidance in order to help humanity achieve all-round wellness. They have many Angel Secrets, which provide a new insight into our challenging situations and matters of the body, mind, heart and soul. The goal and intention of Angel Healing is to bring about great transformations in your life as you journey along the healing path in a loving connection to your personal Guardian Angel. Opening up to all possibilities with trust and the faith that you are supported by the Angel's love will lead you to experience beautiful, amazing miracles in any area of your life. The Angels are ready to make their sacred energy available to you in your time of need, and they will provide guidance each step of the way until you have achieved the results you desire. Angel Healing promotes development on all four levels described below:

∞ Physically: Lead a more fulfilling life, with lasting relationships, successful and purposeful work.

∞ Mentally: Obtain wisdom and higher intelligence, enhanced creativity and a positive perspective.

∞ Emotionally: Feel emotionally balanced, and begin living a life filled with unconditional love and peace.

∞ Spiritually: Become aware of a higher soul-consciousness, and gain guidance towards enlightenment.

The technique of Angel Healing is easy to learn and easy to use. When you call the Angels into your life for healing, they open the doors to your heart so that you can accept their love, and they develop your intuition skills so that you can follow their guidance. Your past is still having an effect in your present moment, and your present state of being will have an effect on your future. By regressing back to identify the causes of unhappiness in your life now, you will be able to create the future you desire. Directing the Angel's healing energy into your body, mind, heart and soul will change your past, present and future on an energetic level, enabling you to think, feel and behave differently and have a much more positive outlook on life. With this outlook, your confidence will lead to happiness in every aspect of your life. The Angel Healing technique will empower you to discover the Angels' Secrets and these will enable you to resolve all challenges, problems or situations you may come across. As your Guardian Angel holds all memories of your past, present and future, it is their role to assist you in every way.

The energy that emanates from Angels is pure unconditional love. It is a shimmery golden ray of light which contains very high vibrations of healing and transmuting properties. Within this gold light, there are beautiful tiny stars which represent the divine intelligence which surpasses human consciousness. In order to help us identify with this healing energy, the Angels have given it the name 'Angel Starlight'. This Angel energy is a remarkable gift for humanity at this time on Earth as it creates blessings of dreams coming true and a life filled with an abundance of love, happiness and well-being. It can be used for absolutely anything, as long as it is with integrity and respect. It works in a mixture of four ways:

∞ Healing Qualities: Angel Starlight provides wonderful qualities such as patience, strength, confidence and many more, all of which are integrated with pure unconditional love, which is the greatest healer. Love for yourself, for others, for your career and for every single area of your life equals healing. During Angel Healing, the Angels guide you to locate your natural, wonderful qualities as they shine their light into your body, mind, heart and soul.

∞ Energy Transmutation: Angel Starlight has alchemical qualities which transform the energy frequencies of other forms of energy and can be directed with the power of your intention. Everything exists on the level of energy, including tangible matter such as the physical body, and intangibles such as thoughts and emotions. During Angel Healing, the Angels guide you to locate and change all forms of energy within your life that are not acting to your benefit, and direct Angel Starlight to transmute their negative energy into positive energy.

∞ Purification: Angel Starlight has cleansing qualities which will purify your life path by removing all obstacles, keeping you away from harmful incidents, accidents, disruptive relationships and anything else that may cause disharmony. During Angel Healing, the Angels purify the flow of your life-force energy by removing the stale and stagnant blocks which create imbalances in your energy levels.

∞ Uniting: Angel Starlight can synchronize and unite all functions within your angelic body. When these are out of sync, the mind and heart are in battle with each other, which causes disruption and disharmony: the soul feels disempowered and disconnected, and the body suffers from disease and disorder. When they are all united, this leads to a wholeness which promotes health and true happiness.

EXERCISE: FEELING ANGEL STARLIGHT ENERGY

PREPARATION

- Set the scene: Clear your space, play soft music, light a candle and hold your meditation crystal.
- Pre-record or have someone read the following guided meditation instructions to you.
- Choose to close your eyes, or keep them open and focus your vision on an object or candle flame.
- Find a comfortable place to lie down for this exercise.

RELAXATION

- Relax your body, heart and mind by taking a deep breath in. Hold, and exhale. Repeat 5–10 times.
- Visualize a stream of golden Angel Starlight energy coming into you, opening all seven chakras into flowers.
- Feel your aura expanding as you gradually become less aware of your physical body.

PRAYER

My Dear Guardian Angel, please help me feel the Angel Starlight and let me receive it into my body, mind, heart and soul. Thank you, with love and gratitude!

THE JOURNEY

- Visualize and feel that your life-force energy is swirling around and within your physical body. Notice any weak areas in your body where the energy is not running through.
- Your Guardian Angel is now kneeling next to you, channelling the golden Angel Starlight energy into your whole body.
- Hold your palms out in front of you and feel the energy building up in your hands. You may experience a tingly or warm sensation in them.
- When you feel ready, place your hands over your heart or any area of your body where you feel there may be an energy block. Hold your hands in this area until you feel the energy flowing into your body.
- As the Angel Starlight merges with your life-force energy, you will start to feel physically, mentally, emotionally and spiritually stronger. Imagine now that the glow around you is much brighter and will be shining through your eyes when you awaken. Brush through your aura with your hands to remove any excess energy around you.

CLOSING DOWN

- Visualize a blue protective light shielding around your aura and each of your seven chakras.
- Spend a moment in gratitude for this healing experience and make a wish to your Guardian Angel.
- Open your eyes and bring your awareness to your physical body. Keep the peace, love and joy you have experienced.
- Direct the Angel Starlight energy into your whole life, into all loved ones and the world.

The techniques of Angel Healing are practised on your angelic body. Your angelic body is your entire being, encompassing the bodies of energy around you as well as your physical anatomy. Your angelic body can be visualized as a huge bubble of light surrounding your physical body with different coloured layers. This bubble of light takes up an enormous amount of space and follows you everywhere. Your whole being is approximately four times the size of your physical body. The healthier the bodies of energy around you are, the healthier you will be physically, as they are all interlinked and work simultaneously. They are all are held in an energy field – your aura.

∞ Etheric Body: This is the first layer of the aura. It holds all the chakras (energy centres) within it, and it is a protective layer, like a shadow, very close to your physical body. Life-force energy runs through this layer and heavily influences your physical health and well-being.

∞ Emotional Body: This is the second layer of the aura. It holds all emotions and feelings within it and it looks like colourful clouds floating around the body. The negative emotions are like dark clouds which filter into your ether body, clogging up your chakras and restricting the life force from running through, and causing disease, disharmony, disorder and the feeling of being disempowered.

∞ Mental Body: This makes up both the third and fourth layers of the aura. It holds within it all mental activity, such as thoughts, beliefs, programmes, memories and patterns of thinking. The third layer is the lower consciousness (logical and limited thinking, or the conscious mind) and the fourth layer is higher consciousness (wisdom and creative thinking, or the subconscious mind).

∞ Soul Body: This is one of the last layers of the aura, and it holds the essence of your spirit, the part of you that is connected to God, oneness or source energy. All spiritual visions filter through this layer into your mental body, where it is translated via intuition into your emotional body to create positive feelings, and then into your physical body, to prompt the relevant actions. Angel Starlight energy will penetrate through this layer and work its way through your aura and into the physical body.

Chakras

Chakras are energy centres held within the aura. They carry your life-force energy through all layers of the angelic body, and determine your ultimate physical well-being. There are seven main chakras, which are aligned from the top of the head to the base of the spine. Chakras can be imagined as roses, as they have layers of petals which open up to be in full blossom or close down like rosebuds. In your natural state, each chakra should be slightly open, and they should all be the same size, and spinning in the same direction at the same speed. During Angel Healing, the chakras are fully open and spin faster as the Angel Starlight runs through them. All chakras govern a function within your body, mind, heart and soul, and they hold memories from the past which affect your well-being, either in a positive or negative manner.

Crown Chakra – Wisdom

This is a beautiful white rose just above the top of your head. This is the home of your soul, a beautiful shining star. The purpose of this chakra is to keep your soul connected to your angelic body and to all that you are. You are able to access the angelic wisdom through this chakra, as it is connected to your subconscious mind. This chakra relates to the pineal gland within the physical body, which controls the melatonin hormones and the nervous system.

Third-Eye Chakra – Intuition

This is a beautiful violet rose in between the eyebrows. This is the home of your intuition or sixth sense; your mind's eye. The purpose of this chakra is to help you to perceive unseen energies such as Angels using your clairvoyant, or psychic, skills. You are able to process and recognize angelic wisdom through this chakra, as it is connected to your conscious mind. It relates to the pituitary gland within the physical body, which controls the growth hormones.

Throat Chakra – Communication

This is a beautiful blue rose in your throat. This is the home of your communication and expression. The purpose of this chakra is to help you to express energy by verbalizing your emotions and thoughts. You are able to listen to and speak the angelic wisdom through this chakra, and this process is also referred to as channelling. It relates to the thyroid gland within the physical body, which controls the metabolism.

Heart Chakra – Unconditional Love

This is a beautiful green rose in the middle of your chest. This is the home of your unconditional love, which looks like a pink centre deep within the chakra. The purpose of this chakra is to feel angelic love and express it through connecting to other hearts in relationships. You are able to extend love, as it manifests from the non-physical to the physical world through this chakra. It relates to the thymus gland and the immune system within the physical body, which determine well-being.

Solar Plexus – Power

This is a beautiful yellow rose in the centre of your stomach. This is the home of your inner power; a golden, bright sphere. The purpose of this chakra is to transmute all negativity into positivity and, through Angel Healing, return you back to your natural state of peace. You are able to locate your power and strength through this chakra. It relates to the pancreas gland and the digestive system within the physical body, which controls the digestion of food, the retention of the good and the removal of the unnecessary.

Sacral Chakra – Creativity

This is a beautiful orange rose slightly below your navel. This is the home of your pleasure. The purpose of this chakra is to express your personality, identity and sexuality by using your creative energy. Angel Healing will remove any unhealthy blocks by transmuting them into confidence, innocence and purity. You are able to access your inner child and connect with children in spirit through this chakra, as all family cords attach from here. It relates to the reproductive glands within the physical body, which control the hormones testosterone and oestrogen.

Root Chakra – Security

This is a beautiful red rose at the base of your spine. This is the home of your physical reality. The purpose of this chakra is to ground your body and awareness of life on Earth. With Angel Healing, you will be able to heighten your consciousness and feel empowered to change from merely having to survive to wanting to achieve. You are able to create your life as you wish it to be through this chakra. It relates to the adrenal glands within the physical body, which control the levels of adrenaline.

Meditation

Meditation is the art of going inwards to understand the true essence of who you really are. When you disconnect with your external world for a short period of time, you are able to connect to your inner world, which consists of your thoughts, values, beliefs, emotions and purpose for living. Through meditation you can shift your consciousness from being negative and limited to access your positive and intelligent higher consciousness in order to change the quality of anything in your life you wish to change.

The process of meditation leads you to a place of peace, and from here you release fear by getting in touch with your inner power to take control. When you go within, you detach from the many external influences imposed upon you which are causing unhappiness.

Meditation aids and complements the process of Angel Healing, as it unites the body, mind, heart and soul and leads to self-realization of your entire being rather than just its physical reality. The Angel Healing Starlight energy is very subtle and can be felt when you are in a deep, relaxed state of meditation. As the energy runs through you, it transmutes negative into positive energy, which will instantly uplift your mood and your outlook on life. During meditation, you can control your mind and focus on using your imagination for creative visualizations. Visualizations help you to connect and communicate with your Angels so that you can receive healing and guidance for your personal growth, and at the same time enhance your natural skills of intuition.

The Secrets of Angel Healing has been designed and structured in such a way that it will boost your powers of intuition, guiding you to perform self-healing exercises using meditation. Many people find it a lot easier to meditate with their eyes closed, therefore you may wish to pre-record and play back the journey of the particular exercise you are working on, leaving sufficient pauses between each step. Alternatively, you could ask someone to read the journey to you very slowly, again leaving enough space between each step, or you could try memorizing the steps in your mind before meditating. The most important factor is to make sure you are in a quiet and clear environment before performing a meditation. I will give you practical instructions on how you can set the scene, clear your mind and relax your body. These instructions should be practised regularly, and soon they will become natural to you.

The practice of meditation brings many benefits:

∞ Physically: Meditation strengthens the immune system and helps boost your natural healing abilities. It regulates blood pressure, and improves blood circulation and energy levels, which will make you look healthier and younger. It also helps you in organizing, controlling and prioritizing all your activities.

∞ Mentally: Meditation balances the left and right hemispheres of the brain, promotes positive thinking and brings you greater control over your thoughts, thereby creating and maintaining lasting peace of mind. Calmness and clarity improves efficiency and your ability to deal with challenging situations.

∞ Emotionally: Meditation removes stress, worry and anxiety and builds self-esteem and confidence, which leads to happiness and joy. This in turn helps you to improve your relationships, while calmness and peaceful emotions will allow you to feel love for yourself, your life and everyone around you.

∞ Spiritually: Meditation brings a connection to higher soul consciousness, opens you up to exploring the unknown and to obtaining guidance from the angelic and spiritual realms. It balances and clears the energy centres within the aura and promotes inner and outer peace, leading to fulfilment and enlightened consciousness.

Preparing to Meditate

Time

It is your choice how much time you wish to dedicate to meditation. The longer you spend practising this stillness, the more it will naturally become part of your daily routine. Many other activities usually take priority over time for meditation. It is important to realize that regular five- or ten-minute meditations are equivalent to a few hours' sleep.

Space

Although you do not really require a sacred place to meditate, it will help you to concentrate and become susceptible to energy if you are in a nice, quiet, clean space. With regular practice, you will naturally learn to switch off from external noise or distractions as you gain and maintain inner peace. Playing soft music, burning incense and lighting a candle can instantly change the energy of your space. Make sure the room temperature is comfortable and that you will not be disturbed by others.

Breathing Exercises

The most challenging aspect of meditation is making yourself relax. By focusing on deep breathing, you take the focus off your thoughts and relax your entire body and emotions. Practise breathing in as slowly and deeply as you can, hold for as long as it is comfortable, and then exhale through the nose or mouth slowly and fully before taking the next deep breath. It is helpful to visualize that you are breathing in positive energy such as love or peace as you exhale the dark, negative energy of stress or tension.

Relaxing Your Body

A brief physical warm-up will loosen your muscles and make meditation more comfortable for you. Start by shaking out your arms and legs, rolling your head from side to side and releasing the tension in your shoulders by bringing them up to your ears and down a few times. Find a comfortable sitting position with your spine straight and your feet firmly on the ground. In this position, you are less likely to fall asleep once you are fully relaxed. If you wish to meditate lying down, place a mat and pillows on the floor or hard surface to keep you grounded. Starting with your feet, tighten your muscles for a few seconds, then release all the tension. Work your way up your body, doing the same for your legs, lower back and hips, abdomen, chest, arms, shoulders, neck and head. As your body starts to relax, there will be a sense of expansion and a feeling that you are no longer actually in your physical body.

Relaxing Your Mind

Allow your thoughts to wander in your mind for a few moments. When you feel ready, repeat in your mind, 'I now let go of my thoughts,' until you have released as much as you can. If you have a few things on your mind which do not seem to want to disappear, recognize that all they want is to be acknowledged. Have a mental list of things that you need to deal with after your meditation. Imagine that, as you acknowledge each one, they are filed in your 'mental filing cabinet'. You will not forget about them and will retrieve them once you are ready to deal with them. As your mind starts to relax, you will reach an altered state of consciousness, just in between being fully awake and nearly drifting off to sleep. This is called the alpha state, and from here you are able to sense the subtle energies of your aura, chakras and the Angels.

Calming Your Emotions

If you are feeling very stressed, it's best to continue taking deep breaths in and out while holding a gem stone such as rose quartz in your hand or over your heart. Focus your attention on your heartbeat as you let go of the negative emotions you are holding within you. Visualize them being placed in a golden pot in front of your heart.

Grounding

Place your feet firmly on the ground and visualize roots emerging from the soles, extending down into the centre of the Earth. This will keep you anchored throughout each meditation and prevent you from feeling light-headed. If you find yourself unbalanced, shaky or rocking, this means you are not properly anchored, so keep imagining your feet being pulled down to the Earth. Another good method is to drink water before, during and after the meditation.

Meditation Journey

You are now ready to meditate and go on an inner journey. You may wish to close your eyes, as it helps to shut off from the external world. It is possible to meditate with your eyes open, by focusing your vision on a particular object, the flame of a candle, for example, or a figurine, flowers, or crystal. Rose quartz crystal has very relaxing and healing properties and also connects with your heart. It is a great tool to use when meditating and connecting with the Angels, as the energy frequency of this crystal is quite high and similar to that of the Angels. When you have used a crystal such as this for some time, you will begin to feel an attachment to it, as it will bear an imprint of both your energy and that of the Angels. (If you want to connect with the angelic realm while you are asleep, place the crystal under your pillow; it will help you to have a restful and peaceful sleep.)

It is best to try meditating both with your eyes closed and open, so that you can find out what you are most comfortable with and what suits you best. Each meditation journey will be different. Once you are prepared to meditate, having followed the steps above, either play back the pre-recorded meditation journey or ask someone to read it to you. Remember that sufficient pauses may be left in between each step. There is no right or wrong way to meditate; it is a very personal thing to each individual. Some people meditate while walking, chanting, singing or listening to music.

Music can play a vital role in meditation as it gives your mind something to focus on and stops it from wandering off into thoughts of other things. In addition, the vibrations of certain instruments will send you into a very deep, relaxed state, and in this state you become more able to sense the subtle energies around you. When choosing music to meditate with, it's best to opt for a purely instrumental soundtrack rather than one with vocals. The practical exercises in this book will give you all the guidance you need. Choose something in which each track lasts a long time, and use the 'repeat' function.

MEDITATION: MEETING YOUR GUARDIAN ANGEL

PREPARATION

- Set the scene: Clear your space, play soft music, light a candle and hold your meditation crystal.
- Pre-record or have someone read the following guided meditation instructions to you.
- Choose to close your eyes, or keep them open and focus your vision on an object or candle flame.

RELAXATION

- Relax your body, heart and mind by taking a deep breath in. Hold, and exhale. Repeat 5–10 times.
- Visualize a stream of golden Angel Starlight energy coming into you, opening all seven chakras into flowers.
- Feel your aura expanding as you gradually become less aware of your physical body.

PRAYER

My Guardian Angel, Thank you for guiding, loving and protecting me. I wish to meet you during this meditation. Please join me now and remain close to me throughout my entire life! Thanking you from my heart.

THE JOURNEY

- Bring your awareness to your heart chakra and see the green petals unfolding one by one until they have transformed into a pink rose. A beautiful, pink path extends out from your heart, paving the way for you to travel towards the Garden of Love.

- Leave your physical body through this pink rose and follow this path. Visualize yourself floating through pink clouds until you find a garden filled with pink and red roses. When you arrive, mentally call your Guardian Angel to your side.

- Little white feathers start falling down into your space as a sign that your Guardian Angel is approaching. A bright, beautiful Angel descends from the pink clouds and comes to stand before you. As your Angel comes closer, notice what your Angel looks like.

- Your Guardian Angel smiles and greets you warmly and tells you a name. Go with the first name that comes into your mind. Notice the feeling of unconditional love and excitement in your heart.

- Enjoy being in the presence of your Guardian Angel. Your Guardian Angel now gives you the emotion of freedom. You are expressing freedom by flying high in the clouds then coming back down, floating through the beautiful flowers. Your energies are now merging together, as you are bonding throughout this experience.

- Have a happy and inspiring conversation with your Guardian Angel about your life path and what your next steps are, before preparing to say goodbye. Walk back through your garden until you find the pink road leading you back to your heart, through the pink rose and into your body.

CLOSING DOWN

- Visualize a blue protective light shielding around your aura, and each of your seven chakras.

- Spend a moment in gratitude for this healing experience and make a wish to your Guardian Angel.
- Open your eyes and bring your awareness to your physical body. Keep the peace, love and joy you have experienced.
- Direct the Angel Starlight energy into your whole life, into all loved ones and the world.

PART III:

CONNECTING AND
COMMUNICATING
WITH ANGELS

Angels are attracted to non-cluttered, peaceful environments. Your outer world reflects what is going on in your internal world, your thoughts and emotions. If you are feeling settled, organized and happy, more than likely the environment you live and work in will reflect this.

Purify your living and work environment by clearing away clutter. This will help you to remove any negativity that may have accumulated over time. The more physical junk you clear away, the more you let go within your heart and mind. You will feel much lighter, more in control and energetic once you discard any items you no longer require, especially if they hold negative memories. Giving items to charity plays a big part in healing, as it is a form of letting go of attachments. It also promotes a healthy balance of giving and receiving, as in letting go of the old, you allow more room for the new to come in. Before giving items to charity, ask your Angels to purify them.

Cleanse the room you have chosen to be your angel sanctuary thoroughly by opening all the windows to allow fresh air and light to flow in. Play some beautiful instrumental music, as this holds purifying, uplifting energy. Burning incense or smudge sticks will remove any stagnant residual energy that has built up. Hold the incense and walk around the room, feeling as you do so an intention of purification. If possible, freshen up the paint on the walls and buy some clean, light curtains and furniture. A wind chime is also a beautiful item to place in your room. It will break up any negative or dense energy that has built up over time.

Within your angel sanctuary, you will build an angelic altar. This will be your shrine for the Angels. By creating a little space in your sanctuary dedicated to your Angels, loving energy will start building, and expand into your whole house. You could convert a dressing table or a chest of drawers into an altar. Decorate it with colours such as pink and lilac which represent love and spiritual evolution. Place upon your Angel altar items which represent love, for example, pictures of loved ones, gem stones, Angel figurines, essential oils and flowers. Angels connect especially to anything related to the essence of rose, especially rose quartz crystal. The items on your altar will hold and vibrate with the energy of love, so they will help to raise the energy of the room and enhance your connection to the Angels. Spending even a few minutes in this sacred place will give you a sense of peace, love and joy as you begin listening to the Angels' guidance and receive their healing.

Intuition

It is essential to have a clear mind when you attempt to connect to your Angels. You cannot stop your mind from thinking, however you can control what you think about. Affirmations are positive statements, and they help you to focus. If, for example, you repeat, 'I am Peace,' or 'I am Love,' eventually you stop thinking about anything else. Take your time with this process and be patient with your mind. If clearing your mind becomes a struggle, focus on a candle flame for a few seconds and take long, deep breaths. As you exhale, visualize your thoughts leaving your mind through your crown chakra, at the top of your head.

Intuition is a natural sense which people are born with. All of us can develop our latent intuition skills with practice. Intuition means going within to see, hear and feel your inner senses. The first intuition skill is clairvoyance, also known as clear-seeing. It is the ability to gain information using the mind's eye, or third eye. By using this skill regularly and practising the meditations in this book, you will be able to perceive the subtle energies around you, such as Angels.

The second intuition skill is clairaudience, also known as clear-hearing. It is the ability to tune into different frequency waves. By listening to the messages from your Angels by completing the exercises in this book, you will begin to be able to distinguish between your own inner voice and the angelic guidance you are receiving.

The third intuition skill is clairsentience, also known as clear-feeling. It is the ability to feel other subtle energies as you raise or lower your own energy frequency through relaxation or meditation. This is often experienced as having a gut instinct or hunch about something or someone.

Practice makes perfect when you are trying to communicate with the Angels. Remove your doubts and trust that you are making progress. The meditation below has been designed to help you exercise all of the above intuition skills.

MEDITATION: CONNECTING WITH THE ANGELS

PREPARATION

- Set the scene: Clear your space, play soft music, light a candle and hold your meditation crystal.
- Pre-record or have someone read the following guided meditation instructions to you.
- Choose to close your eyes, or keep them open and focus your vision on an object or candle flame.

RELAXATION

- Relax your body, heart and mind by taking a deep breath in. Hold, and exhale. Repeat 5–10 times.
- Visualize a stream of golden Angel Starlight energy coming into you, opening all seven chakras into flowers.
- Feel your aura expanding as you gradually become less aware of your physical body.

PRAYER

- Angels of Intuition, please connect with me now and help me to develop my intuition skills. Thank you!

THE JOURNEY

- Visualize a beautiful purple rose opening on your forehead, in between your eyebrows. As it blossoms, you see a stunning purple eye coming through, with light shining through it.
- An Angel of Intuition is standing in front of you. It has white, gold and purple light all around its aura. The Angel now places golden Angel Starlight into your third eye, clearing away any dark clouds.
- Listen to the three words of wisdom that the Angel of Intuition is going to give you. Trust that what comes into your mind is from the Angel and not from your mind.
- Angels love musical instruments such as harps and sometimes use the energy of sound to direct their messages to you. Listen to the relaxing and Heavenly music being played to you and trust that what you hear is a personal greeting for you from the angelic realm.
- Feel the energy now running through your whole body. Notice any changes in the room temperature or around your body. You may experience warm energy or tingly sensations within your heart.
- As the exercise comes to an end, see, hear and feel yourself expressing your love and gratitude to the Angel, and express the happiness and joy that you have made a connection.

CLOSING DOWN

- Visualize a blue protective light shielding your aura and each of your seven chakras.
- Spend a moment in gratitude for this experience and make a wish to your Guardian Angel.
- Open your eyes and bring your awareness to your physical body. Keep the peace, love and joy you have experienced.
- Direct the Angel Starlight energy into your whole life, into all loved ones and the world.

Channelling

Channelling is the art of bringing information from one realm of existence to another, for instance from the angelic realm to the Earth realm. Another form of channelling is the transfer of information between your creative, subconscious mind into your logical, conscious mind. When channelling messages from the Angels, the information enters through your crown chakra at the top of your head, through to your ears so you can hear the information, to your throat so you can speak the information, to your heart so you can feel the message, and to your legs so you can take action!

Through prayer, you talk to the Angels; through meditation, you listen. The more you speak to your Angels, the more effective your prayers will become. Each time you communicate, your relationship grows stronger and you begin to integrate their energy with your own. Whether you choose to communicate out loud or in your mind, the Angels will still hear you. Pour your heart out to your Guardian Angel, an Archangel or any other Angel and explain the situation with which you need help. Remember that Angels are divine messengers. They will answer your prayers to the highest and best good of all involved.

Meditation is a tool that you can use to quieten your mind, to allow you to listen to the guidance of the Angels. Our minds and lives are usually so busy we don't take the opportunity to stop and relax. If we do, we can explore the unknown or find the answers to our problems. Making the decision to meditate a little each day will help you to strengthen your relationship with the Angels. Meditation will not only have positive benefits on your physical well-being, but is also the way to communicate with your Guardian Angel. Everything you experience in a meditation will be held within your hidden subconscious mind, and fragments of what you have experienced will filter through slowly to your conscious mind. If you are able to remember what you have experienced during your meditation when you return to full consciousness, it is advisable to write down as much as you can in your journal.

Creative Writing

The best way to communicate with your Guardian Angel through writing is to begin by writing down your emotions, then write about the challenges you are faced with, and then ask the Angels for guidance and advice. Once you have finished writing, close your eyes and visualize your Guardian Angel standing behind you. Feel its wings wrapped around your body. Just becoming aware that the Angels are in your space will raise your consciousness and make you feel more positive and inspirational. The Angels will telepathically communicate their loving messages through you. Listen to them. When you feel ready to write, put pen to paper and allow the words to flow and your hand to move over the page.

The speed of this communication may vary, so be patient if the flow of information is slow. Take care not to think too much, as it will block the energy. Sometimes the flow can be very rapid, with so much information coming through that you are unable to control your hand. Go with the motion and trust that this is information being passed through from the higher realms. You will know that it is not coming from your conscious mind because the words will be overwhelmingly positive and inspirational. The words will not be those you would usually say to yourself. Angels have a different manner of speaking, and they often start with 'Dear child' or 'Dear loved one'.

The flow of writing will come naturally to an end. If you find that you are unable to achieve Angel writing, the reason may be that you are focusing too much on what is going to happen and your logical, conscious mind is taking control. The most important thing to remember when attempting Angel writing is to have intention, trust and faith.

Angel Signs

Angels vibrate at a different frequency to those of us on Earth, so it takes time and effort to bring us physical signs. Angels will try to reach out to you by lowering their frequency as you raise yours in order to feel their presence. Angels understand that as people start to open up to the angelic realm, their logical mind will seek some form of validation or 'proof'. The Angels will lovingly give you a sign that they have heard your prayers, but they ask that you do not specify exactly what you want!

Angels are very considerate and will take into account any fears you may have about using your skills of intuition. For example, they will not appear suddenly in your mind's eye and frighten you. Their communication will start with very subtle messages, and as your intuition develops, the messages will become louder and clearer. If you love to be tickled, the Angels will know this and will probably give you a tickling sensation as a sign. It can take anything from a few days to many years for you to notice the signs, and to be reassured that it is the Angels who are sending them. Some of the most common Angel signs are:

∞ White feathers: These may be appearing in unusual places or fall down into your path as you are thinking about Angels or after you have prayed to them.

∞ Sparkling stars: These may be of any colour, but especially they appear as little sparkles of white light. They will flash very quickly and will only register in your mind for a fraction of a second. Don't worry if you are unable to see them for long.

∞ Music and song lyrics: This is a way the Angels use to catch your attention when they are trying to get a message through. When you hear a certain type of music or a song that connects with your heart, say a little thank-you to your Angel.

∞ People: In emergency situations, people may miraculously appear to offer you a helping hand. This is an example of Angels being verbally channelled to you through others.

∞ Miracles: These are happening at each and every moment in your life. Each prayer is heard and answered in ways which may seem unlikely or even impossible, due to the time and space restrictions on Earth. Angels do not suffer the same restrictions, so they can find a solution to the difficulties you face, and answers to your prayers.

Angel Card Readings

Angel cards are a perfect way for you to answer any questions you may have and to give you an insight into how your past is influencing your present moment, and how your present actions will influence your future. If this is the insight you seek, the Angel card reading will take the form of a three-card past, present, future spread. There are many other spreads that you can use, and you can create spreads yourself.

When reading cards, it is important to clear your aura from external influences and open up your chakras to allow the angelic wisdom to flow through you. Close your eyes for a few moments and connect with your Guardian Angel. Ask your question out loud or say a little prayer. After shuffling the cards, use your intuitive 'feeling' to pull out the cards most relevant to your question. Your intuition will also tell you how many cards are needed to answer your question. Once you lay the cards out in front of you, combine the message you are telepathically hearing from your Guardian Angel with the pictures and words on the card.

MEDITATION: COMMUNICATING WITH THE ANGELS

PREPARATION

- Set the scene: Clear your space, play soft music, light a candle and hold your meditation crystal.
- Pre-record or have someone read the following guided meditation instructions to you.
- Choose to close your eyes, or keep them open and focus your vision on an object or candle flame.

RELAXATION

- Relax your body, heart and mind by taking a deep breath in. Hold, and exhale. Repeat 5–10 times.
- Visualize a stream of golden Angel Starlight energy coming into you, opening all seven chakras into flowers.
- Feel your aura expanding as you gradually become less aware of your physical body.

PRAYER

My Guardian Angel, I ask that you connect with me now. Please show me how I can best communicate with the angelic realm and enhance my natural intuition skills. Thank you, with love and gratitude!

THE JOURNEY

- Visualize a beautiful Angel of Communication with blue light surrounding it sitting next to you at your angelic altar. Affirm to yourself: 'I am clairvoyant,' and be patient, remembering to relax your body and mind.

- Listen to the inspirational message that this Angel of Communication has for you regarding how to communicate with your Angels in future. Feel angelic energy pass over your ears, activating your ear chakras. You may hear a word such as 'trust' or 'patience'. Affirm to yourself: 'I am clairaudient.'

- Feel the energy coming from the Angel of Communication running through your heart and spreading around your entire body. Ask a question regarding anything in your life and feel the answer through your emotions. Affirm: 'I am clairsentient.'

CLOSING DOWN

- Visualize a blue protective light shielding around your aura and each of your seven chakras.

- Spend a moment in gratitude for this experience and make a wish to your Guardian Angel.

- Open your eyes and bring your awareness to your physical body. Keep the peace, love and joy you have experienced.

- Direct the Angel Starlight energy into your whole life, into all loved ones and the world.

PART IV:

ARCHANGELS

Archangel Michael

Warrior Angel:	'He who is like God'
Keywords:	Protection/Strength/Courage
Chakra:	Throat

Michael is known as the Manager of all Angels. His role is to oversee the world and act as the warrior by escorting away lower energies and bringing protection. Using a sword of energy, he clears home and work environments and seals them with angelic protective light. Michael works closely with light workers, who have as their mission the spreading of angelic energies through healing and communication.

Archangel Michael is thought of as the greatest of all Angels throughout the world and in many religions. These are the benefits he brings to your body, mind, heart and soul:

Body

∞ To strengthen the body, mind, heart and soul connection.

∞ To guide towards positive lifestyle changes so that you become happier.

∞ To protect and keep you safe in your home or work environment.

Mind

∞ To clear the mind from cluttered and negative thoughts.

∞ To help in keeping your thoughts positive with affirmations.

∞ To remove stress, worry and anxiety in the mind.

Heart

∞ To cut negative cords which no longer serve in a positive way.

∞ To give you courage when speaking your truth about feelings.

∞ To enable you to be clear about what you desire in a relationship.

Soul

∞ To clear away psychic attacks and release spirit attachments.

∞ To give courage when overcoming difficult life lessons.

∞ To inspire and guide all light workers and Angel Healers.

My Experience with Archangel Michael

Archangel Michael first appeared to me during a self-healing meditation. I was in need of strength and power to move forward from a difficult situation in my life. I needed to be in a place where I could be free, however I felt restricted by the many difficult obstacles in my path. I had read about Michael's presence being very powerful and that he specialized in cutting away anything negative within or around our lives, using his holy sword. Before my meditation, I set the intention to connect with his energy but cleared my mind of any expectations of what I should or should not see. I remember the darkness in my mind, as I had my eyes closed, and I was falling deeper into a relaxed state when I began to see something unusual. I focused on what seemed like sparkles of blue light in the very far distance. As I focused, these sparkles of light formed into a spiralling ball which was travelling towards me, becoming larger as it did so. It stopped getting bigger when it was the size of a tennis ball, and blue energy emanated from it as thousands of blue stars came towards me, washing over my whole body. My eyes began to flicker as the energy hit my face. It felt incredible. From my face, it moved down to my throat, and I literally felt as if I was drinking this energy! I felt my throat was physically expanding. Although I didn't hear it, I knew and believed that this was Michael's energy, and he was giving me his wisdom and the confidence to speak my truth.

Nowadays, when I call for Michael to intervene in any personal situations or during healing sessions, he appears in my mind as a very large, tall, handsome Angel with beautiful blue and golden wings. Michael has protected me, and many people I know and love, many times. One specific situation I remember was when I was walking home at night. I came across a group of drunken people who were looking for a fight. I was very fearful of their negative energy, and so I immediately called upon Michael's energy for protection and visualized that he was energetically standing behind me, covering me with his blue cloak. Within a few moments of me imagining this, the group's attention was diverted, and they all moved out of my path.

I ask Archangel Michael, with so much love and gratitude, to continue to protect us all from harm, to guard our homes and loved ones, as he can be everywhere with everyone simultaneously. I am forever grateful to him for helping me to find my voice and speak my truth. In doing so, I have overcome my severe shyness and have realized that, whereas throughout my whole life I have struggled with communication, it seems that communication – channelling the Angels' wisdom – was always destined to be my strongest tool and gift.

Message from Archangel Michael

I am the Guardian of your Earth and its inhabitants. I watch over the Guardian Angels to ensure that they are lovingly and willingly fulfilling their purpose in guiding you beautiful souls towards the light. I am always around helping to clear the pollution from your planet and vacuuming away the darkness. I am hopeful that very soon the light which is being bestowed upon humanity at this time is growing more and more as we move you along the path towards Ascension. I work closely with my many colleagues within the angelic hierarchy and appear by your side when you call upon any of us for assistance. Our divine mission is to serve our mighty creator and our divine joy is seeing the results of your happiness and evolution. You are as powerful as the universe that holds you, and it is time for you all to remember your individual power, yet hold hands together with others as you all rejoice in the abundance of your desires. Your life is magnificent, and your light work is spreading the love and joy of your angelic selves.

Archangel Raphael

Healing Angel:	'God heals'
Keywords:	Healing/Intuition/Wholeness
Chakra:	Third Eye

Raphael's role is to guide and assist people involved in the healing professions, such as doctors, counsellors, practitioners and scientists. He also helps to develop intuition centres within the body. These are the benefits he brings to your body, mind, heart and soul:

Body

∞ To clear blocks within the angelic body, aura and chakras.

∞ To aid healing of all physical, mental, emotional and spiritual difficulties.

∞ To enhance natural intuitive and channelling abilities.

Mind

∞ To release fears around being a professional healer.

∞ To help maintain a positive outlook regarding your health.

∞ To use positive affirmations about your healing abilities.

Heart

∞ To heal a broken heart and the wounds of past relationships.

∞ To aid with self-forgiveness and forgiving others.

∞ To spread love into other people's lives.

Soul

∞ To assist with repairing the soul to feel whole again.

∞ To help you feel spiritually connected as well as grounded.

∞ To increase soul consciousness and channel angelic wisdom.

My Experience with Archangel Raphael

This beautiful Archangel appeared by my side while I was giving a healing session. At the time, I wasn't aware of Angel Starlight, but I had read about the Archangels. I visualized Raphael in very flowing robes and with long, curly hair. His hands are so full of energy, so slender and long; one hand is long enough to cover my whole head. Archangel Raphael is the Angel of vision and intuition. He activated my third-eye chakra so that I could intuitively see energy and how it moves around bodies.

My experience of opening this chakra was amazing. I visualized a beautiful purple eye and felt a stretching sensation in my forehead as it opened. My eyes were flickering very fast, and they slightly turned upwards, still remaining closed. From that moment onwards, I knew that my psychic clairvoyance was enhanced and that my healing sessions would be a lot more effective. Archangel Raphael showed me that I was in control of this psychic awareness, and that I could close my third-eye chakra whenever I wanted.

It took time and practice for me to consciously remember what to do, but nowadays, just my intention to open or close it works within seconds.

Message from Archangel Raphael

Wholeness comes from oneness. Acceptance comes from gentleness. Be very gentle with yourselves, dear loved ones. The strings of your heart are pulled when you follow your instincts for moving towards happiness. You are very wise, old beings in new, young bodies, and we guide you to remember your wisdom. Dedicate a promise to yourselves that you will not let this opportunity pass you by without accomplishing your soul's missions. You have too much to give and offer each other. Sharing is a very beautiful practice and will always lead you towards creating more abundance in your lives, not lack. As you all, one by one, open your minds and hearts to the truth of love, your world will become a better place to live in. Hold hands with your neighbour; declare love, not war. Declare oneness, not separation. Show appreciation to all those who come your way and play a role in teaching your life lessons. I am the Angel of travel, and I lovingly help you to move forward and physically explore your beautiful world. Ask me to watch over your plans of movement. Let us now affirm that everything is working perfectly in your life. Until you wish to call upon the subtle, gentle energy of your dear light beings, we wish you to receive all that you deserve.

Archangel Chamuel

Love Angel:	'He who sees God'
Keywords:	Unconditional Love/ Relationships/ Peace
Chakra:	Heart

Chamuel's role is to bring the principle of pure unconditional love into people's lives in all forms and areas of their lives. The main areas are relationships, family, career and social life. Chamuel helps us to love ourselves unconditionally and project this into every area; he also brings comfort and peace to those who are mourning loved ones or failed relationships, and helps you to move forward by attracting a soul mate. These are the benefits he brings to your body, mind, heart and soul:

Body

∞ To heal problems or illnesses related to the heart, e.g. heart disease.

∞ To remove stress and tension from the body and bring inner peace.

∞ To guide towards unconditionally accepting yourself and others.

Mind

∞ To clear negative thoughts creating stress, guilt or shame.

∞ To help maintain a loving outlook on life, love and romance.

∞ To assist in understanding partners' thought patterns and beliefs.

Heart

∞ To clear blocks around unconditional love for yourself and others.

∞ To heal your broken heart, loneliness and betrayal of the heart.

∞ To strengthen hope and faith regarding unconditional love.

Soul

∞ To assist with grieving for lost loved ones or ex-partners.

∞ To attract soul mates and twin souls in divine timing.

∞ To understand the soul's purpose and all love relationships.

My Experience with Archangel Chamuel

This beautiful Archangel is filled with pink unconditional love energy, and it radiates from his aura. He helps those who are searching for love and romance and will be there to comfort those who have lost love. I was in both these situations for many years. Every time I meditated on love, I would see bright shades of pink unconditional love energy swirling around me. I believe it was this Archangel who guided me towards my soul mates and helped me to experience true love. I see Chamuel as a very peaceful, smiling Angel surrounded by little baby Angels (cupids, or cherubs). Each time there is a call for romance, I see Chamuel directing these love Angels to intervene in the person's romantic or love life.

Message from Archangel Chamuel

Dear loved ones, I hear your cries for love. Whether it is self-love, loving another or your wanting to be loved, I understand and have much compassion. It is sad to say, there is a lack of love in many lives; this is because of the illusion of fear. The secret of having love in all forms is to love fearlessly. No matter what your past experiences, or what you have witnessed of others' unsuccessful relationships, do not dwell on negative thoughts or give up on love. Once you give up on love, you give on yourselves, as you are love. Open your hearts to receive without guilt. Learn not to judge others, and learn that where there is love, there is peace. When peace is not present, there are conditions attached to the purity of love. I love you.

Archangel Gabriel

Messenger Angel:	'God is my strength'
Keywords:	Career/Communication/ Life Purpose/Purification
Chakra:	Sacral and Base

Gabriel's role is to bring messages from Heaven and to help people to find their true calling on Earth. These are the benefits he brings to your body, mind, heart and soul:

Body

∞ To purify the physical body of all toxins.

∞ To help clear blocks regarding sexuality.

∞ To express sexuality, identity and creativity.

Mind

∞ To purify the mind of impure thoughts.

∞ To assist with leadership and using power.

∞ To help with career changes and transitions.

Heart

∞ To purify the heart of bitter emotions.

∞ To open the heart to all possibilities and miracles in life.

∞ To resolve conflict between family members.

Soul

∞ To help communication with spirit guides, soul family & children in spirit.

∞ To enhance channelling abilities through creative writing, speaking and reading cards.

∞ To awaken your life mission and soul's purpose.

My Experience with Archangel Gabriel

This beautiful Archangel played a big part in helping me to write this book. Writing a book, like any other creative project, is very time-consuming and requires patience, organization and focus. Archangel Gabriel is the creative Archangel, and he helped me to balance many projects and work commitments by prioritizing my time and energy effectively. He would constantly remind me to set the Heavenly scene and to be in the right frame of mind before channelling information. At times, I would have writer's block, and he would sit by my side, taking me into a deep meditation to allow the Angel Starlight to flow through and cleanse me. This always worked perfectly, and I would feel inspired to continue writing.

Message from Archangel Gabriel

You are all writers and all have a story to tell which will inspire your fellow companions, friends and the rest of the world. If only you would take time to appreciate the wonderful journeys of self-development you have made and the many golden opportunities which are constantly presenting themselves to you. Healing allows you to express your divinity in any form. Whether it's through dance, art, writing or designing, each person has a unique talent to share with the world. See the good in everyone, encourage each other to have confidence and belief in your abilities. Life is about living, living is about exploring and exploring comes from passion. Follow your passion, and don't be frightened to bring it into your life as your career. Passion leads to abundance, as people rejoice and believe in your product when you do. Mundane work drains the life force from your body, mind, heart and soul, leaving you not only unfulfilled but despondent. This leads to regrets in your future, which consequently creates a negative outlook on yourself and your life. Change is the way forward. Ask for angelic guidance to take the necessary steps, risks and action to follow your dreams and bring them into your reality. Blessings and love from your messenger.

MEDITATION: VISITING THE ARCHANGELS' SANCTUARY

PREPARATION

- Set the scene: Clear your space, play soft music, light a candle and hold your meditation crystal.
- Pre-record, or have someone read the following guided meditation instructions to you.
- Choose to close your eyes, or keep them open and focus your vision on an object or candle flame.

RELAXATION

- Relax your body, heart and mind. Ground yourself and connect to your soul, the sparkling star.
- Visualize the Angel Starlight energy running through your body, opening all seven chakras into flowers.
- Feel your aura expanding as you gradually become less aware of your physical body.

THE JOURNEY

- You are about to go on a journey above your space to meet the Archangels.
- Visualize your soul star rising above your body and becoming large enough to hold you in. There is a strong silver cord attached from your soul to your physical body, which will always keep you connected to the Earth.
- As you ascend higher and higher, you pass the sun, stars, universe and the spiritual realm until you arrive in the angelic realm. You will know when you have arrived when you feel like you are floating in clouds and your heart feels so much love and joy.
- Archangel Michael greets you in a beautiful room of different shades of vibrant blue. You see that he is standing there like a

bodyguard of the angelic realm, yet very closely connected to the Earth. He invites you into his sanctuary and begins to cut your negative cords using his large sword of energy. Feel him giving you the strength and courage to overcome your fears about connecting with Angels. Continue to ascend higher after saying goodbye to Michael.

- Archangel Raphael's sanctuary is the colour of emerald green. It looks like a healing room with a therapy couch and soft angelic music playing in the background. He greets you and invites you to lie on his healing couch. Feel him showering you with Angel Starlight and uniting your body, mind, heart and soul to make you feel complete wholeness. Continue to ascend higher after saying goodbye to Raphael.

- Archangel Chamuel's sanctuary is the colour of rose-pink. Heart bubbles and baby Angels playfully float around in it. You are approached by this Angel, and he invites you to play with the little ones. The feeling of dancing and being playful brings much joy and happiness into your heart. He now asks you to let go of seriousness and embrace your inner child as you pamper yourself in this joyous way. You are now as free as an Angel and will take the feelings of peace and harmony along with you on your journey. Continue to ascend higher after saying goodbye to Chamuel.

- Archangel Gabriel's sanctuary is golden and has many steps which lead you towards the enlightenment of your body, mind, heart and soul. After floating up higher, you reach two very large golden doors. These doors open for you, and you are greeted by Gabriel. You notice that he is holding a horn, which he uses to bring you a beautiful message from your creator and give you the sounds of divine wisdom. He now guides you along a few more steps, to stand before two more golden doors. As these doors open, you are shown your true life purpose and how to use your creativity in your career.

- The other Archangels now join you to wish you well in your life. You now give gratitude for the guidance and healing energies that they will be providing in your life from this moment onwards.
- Visualize yourself back in your large star and travel back down into your body, passing through the different sanctuaries and realms, through the stars and descending back to Earth, back into your body through your crown chakra.

CLOSING DOWN

- Visualize a blue protective light shielding your aura and each of your seven chakras.
- Spend a moment in gratitude for this healing experience and make a wish to your Guardian Angel.
- Open your eyes and bring your awareness to your physical body. Keep the peace, love and joy you have experienced.
- Direct the Angel Starlight energy into your whole life, to your loved ones and the world.

PART V:

ANGEL HEALING
FOR THE BODY

This chapter will cover some of the physical challenges that people are faced with throughout their lives, especially with regards to health and well-being. There will be a short description of the problem and of the way in which it is usually caused. The advice I relate here has been directly channelled from the Angels and will therefore provide you with a completely different perspective on the situation under discussion. After each section, there is an Angel Healing meditation which will begin to release blocks on an energetic level. The practical exercises give an idea of what action should be taken, and affirmations for the mind will enhance your healing by changing your thought patterns into positivity.

The natural state of the body is to function properly, with all systems working in sync with each other. Your body is the temple of your soul, the cage of your heart and the vehicle of your mind. Your health and well-being depend on the balance of your mind, heart and soul. In Angel Healing, we believe that the physical body acts as a mirror of your thoughts and emotions and reflects whatever may not be working properly, making you aware of the problem so that you are able to address it. When you begin to take control of your inner world, this will shine through into your outer world through your physical body, giving you higher levels of energy, happiness and good health. Angel Healing offers solutions to the physical effects you are experiencing by treating their original causes.

On a soul level, as part of your life journey, you may have chosen to experience certain illnesses or health challenges in order to overcome them with your willpower and courage. When these challenges present themselves, people tend to have more appreciation for life and for the smallest opportunities to experience love, happiness and good health. Guardian Angels will ask you to look deeper into your physical symptoms, and change your focus from negative to positive. Everything you hold within and around you is a form of energy, and negative energy has a tendency to build up and may manifest itself within your body as pain, disorder or illness. Your angelic body consists of your entire being, including your physical anatomy. Everything is interlinked, therefore when one thing is out of balance, it will have an effect on the others.

Through Angel Healing, you can use Angel Starlight to transmute the negative energies held deep within the body, rather than hiding or ignoring them. Energy remains in the form it is in until you choose to change it into another form which will be of much more benefit to your well-being. Positive thinking is a great way of beginning your healing, however, although it will have positive influences, it will not treat or heal the physical problem from the core, the actual cause of your physical symptoms. For instance, if you suffer from stress and it manifests within your body as migraines, you can temporarily heal the symptoms with painkillers, however, the next time something triggers stress within you, your migraine will come back. Learning how to remove the cause of stress and how to control your emotions will permanently heal the migraines. Angel Healing gives you the support, energy and focus to find the recurring patterns and to eliminate them, using healing, transmuting and purifying Angel Starlight energy.

The Angels will also help you to have the patience to see the healing process through. In the Earth realm, we live in a world of duality: the positive cannot exist without the negative. However, in the angelic realm, there is only one pure form of energy: love. Even though we are in physical bodies, Angels believe that love can cure any problem and heal any pain. We need to start by loving the body, by ceasing to punish it and by learning not to take advantage of the intelligent machine that carries our mind, heart and soul. We are blessed in so many ways by having all these miraculous functions working in perfect order to give us the breath of life. A healthy body comes from a healthy mind, heart and soul. Connect with and acknowledge each organ, bone, system, function and every other part within your physical anatomy now, and direct love into them as you visualize the golden Angel Starlight shining through and revitalizing them.

Angel Healing is a complementary therapy for medical conditions. Taking time to love your body inside and out with sheer gratitude is the Angels' medicine for lasting health and well-being.

Illness

Disease

'Disease' is the opposite of being at ease. The cause of disease may be an energetic block stopping the flow of your natural life-force energy. An imbalance in the angelic body caused by negativity may also manifest as disease. The effects of these will be exhibited through many different symptoms. Angels will clear these blocks with Angel Starlight energy so that the body can restore its natural flow of energy through maximizing the efficiency of your immune system. They will also restore the harmony and peace between all the levels of your existence. There are many different ways of diagnosing disease, and these have a variety of names and symptoms. The Angels will provide guidance and healing on the cause, which may be held on any level, but without focusing too much on the medical diagnosis itself.

Discomfort

The physical body experiences pain when there is a build-up of stagnant energy within your angelic body. When the chakras become blocked, your life-force energy is unable to flow through them with ease, and this causes tension within the body. Many people rely on certain painkillers to alleviate pain, and taking them becomes a natural part of their everyday life. Angels will direct Angel Starlight healing energy into the area of your discomfort through the corresponding chakra in order to clear the blockages that are causing a build-up of energy in that area. The cause of your pain may be held on a different part of your angelic body, such as the negative beliefs within the mental body, an accumulation of negative emotions within the emotional body, or negative karma within the spiritual body. Angel Healing will aim to heal the causes and effects of your discomfort.

Disorder

Certain disorders manifest within the body due to a lack of order within your inner world. One disorder in particular that Angels can help you understand is Obsessive Compulsive Disorder. In Angel Healing, the Angels guide you to recognize your obsessions and their causes. Compulsions are actions which are carried out because of your obsessions; these are the effects of the disorder. With the help of the Angels, you will identify the underlying fear and negative belief programmes that lie behind your OCD, and with Angel Starlight energy these can be transformed into positivity. This will gradually break up unhealthy patterns of behaviour and rituals of compulsive actions. During meditation, your Angel will give you confidence to overcome your disorders.

Distant Healing

As the Angels exist on a realm that is not limited by our physical restrictions, they are able to be in many places at the same time. If you are aware of someone who needs Angel Healing, you can ask the Angels to channel Angel Starlight energy and direct it with your consciousness to the person, situation or place where it is required. To enhance this healing technique, you could choose to go into a meditative state, where your brainwaves are altered to alpha state; in this state you will feel the healing energy coming through your body, then travelling through the universe to where it is needed. Visualizing Angels surrounding the person in need and filling their space with golden Angel Starlight energy will strengthen this healing process. It is beneficial to arrange a certain time with the person to whom you are directing Angel Healing so that they can prepare themselves and be in an appropriately relaxed state to accept the energy.

Dependence

Addictions are cravings for a reconnection to your soul. There is a deep yearning within us to feel and live in a blissful state, to deny anything that is negative in your reality, and this is only achieved through an altered state of mind and a shift of energy within the body. Meditation is a positive and healthy form of achieving this ecstatic state as it connects you to your soul without harming you in any way. Any form of self-destructive behaviour done in excess in order to alter the state of your consciousness will only temporarily create the state of bliss required. It is a way of numbing out the pain of the disconnection between your body, mind, heart and soul.

Any pleasurable feeling achieved from any addiction is stored within the subconscious mind as a positive memory and creates a mental programme that tells you that the addiction is good for you and is serving you well and bringing many benefits. These programmes then become your patterns of behaviour, or habits, and will eventually cause an imbalance of your chakras, weaken your aura and may manifest as disease in your body.

Angel Healing can be used to treat the deeply embedded causes of your addictions. As the reason behind any addiction is to achieve an altered state of consciousness, the practice of meditation will slowly remove the need for any substance addiction by itself providing an altered state of consciousness. During meditation, your Guardian Angel will connect you with your soul, a connection that is essential to your healing and transformation. When you are connected to your soul, this will enhance the connection between your emotional and mental bodies, and you will feel whole, empowered and that you are being fully supported in your efforts to conquer your addiction. You will go on an inner journey to identify the mental programmes that are sending signals throughout your nervous system in your body and making you believe you have cravings for the substance.

Your Guardian Angel will also repair and strengthen your entire angelic body so that you are strong enough to overcome your addiction. When you are ready to face the truth and the cause of your addiction and to heal the effects of your addictions, your Guardian Angel will help you to bring the negative energies within you to the surface in order to release them permanently. The Angels will help you to observe your addictive behaviours, without making any judgement upon you. By observing your thoughts, your emotions and your actions, you will know that each is a result of your past memories. You are now empowered to change these into positivity in your present moment through willpower. By doing so, you set yourself free from negativity and create health and well-being for your future.

ANGEL HEALING MEDITATION FOR ILLNESS

ANGEL SECRET:

'Illness is an illusion.
Vitality is your reality.'

CROWN CHAKRA

Angel Starlight enters your angelic body through a beautiful white rose just above your physical body. You see a silvery sparkling star in the centre of your crown chakra and connect with your soul. Your Guardian Angel now guides you to place your palms facing up and held slightly above your body. The Angel Starlight healing energy is filling your palms, and you sense a warm, tingly feeling in your hands.

THIRD-EYE CHAKRA

Angel Starlight travels down into the purple rose between your two eyes and into your mind. It now begins to clear your intuition blocks. Your Guardian Angel now teaches you how to do an intuitive scan of your entire angelic body, beginning with your physical body. The Angel Starlight energy runs down from your crown chakra into your third eye, activating your intuition X-ray vision. Starting from your feet and slowly working your way upwards, you look beyond the surface of your body. Looking deeper into and around each organ, try to locate any dark or dense areas.

THROAT CHAKRA

Angel Starlight travels down into the blue rose in your throat and extends towards your ears. Ask your Guardian Angel to help you to communicate with your body so that you can intuitively understand what is lacking or what is not functioning correctly. Lovingly speak to each organ, limb and other part of your body individually. Now give thanks to each part of your body, including your nervous, immune, digestive and endocrine systems for the purpose they serve, and to your spine for supporting you.

HEART CHAKRA

Angel Starlight travels down into the green rose within your heart and, as it blossoms, you see that it slowly transforms into a pink rose. Your Guardian Angel now guides your palms over each chakra, starting from your crown chakra, allowing the built-up healing energy to be channelled into your body. Feel intuitively guided as to how long each chakra needs. Then place your palms on the darker areas on your physical body which you found in the scanning exercise. Visualize the golden Angel Starlight now being circulated around your whole body internally, along with your blood, purifying all cells, organs, muscles and bones.

SOLAR PLEXUS CHAKRA

Angel Starlight travels down into the yellow rose within your stomach area, the core of your being. It now extends out into your emotional, mental, and spiritual bodies, cleansing and purifying all thoughts and emotions regarding your well-being. Your Guardian Angel now strengthens and unites your body, mind, heart and soul.

SACRAL CHAKRA

Angel Starlight travels down into the orange rose just below your navel and activates your creative abilities. Visualize the beautiful, large Archangel Raphael now standing behind you with his energetic healing hands at your crown chakra, channelling an emerald-green light through your body, which now merges with the golden Angel Starlight. His healing energy alleviates all disorders, diseases and discomforts within your body. Give thanks to Archangel Raphael as he finishes by grounding you on the Earth and removing all excess energy from around you.

ROOT CHAKRA

Angel Starlight travels down into the red rose at the base of your spine. Your Guardian Angel now brings your hands together into prayer position, which stops the Angel Starlight from flowing through them. Say a prayer to your Guardian Angel regarding your health and well-being and that of all your loved ones. Visualize beautiful white Angel dust now falling from the sky above and removing all impurities on Earth.

Success Story

Hattie came for Angel Healing for help with her thyroid imbalance disorder. During her meditation, the Angels explained that she had been suppressing her thoughts and feelings throughout her life because she was afraid of confrontation. She chose to hold her deepest and saddest emotions hidden within her instead of releasing them by speaking her truth. This had a negative impact and created a block within her throat chakra, which affected the thyroid gland and nervous system. As the healing energy started flowing through her body and chakras, Archangel Michael gave her the energy of courage to speak out about her hidden thoughts and feelings, especially towards those who had upset or hurt her. She found this emotional release quite difficult to begin with. She continued to speak out about all the injustices she felt had been perpetrated on her, about her own regrets, her guilt and many other things. Eventually, her confidence grew, as she was now visualizing people in her meditation, and they were coming to her and listening to what she had to say. She even heard people apologizing to her and asking her to forgive them. By this stage in her Angel Healing, all barriers to communication had been broken down and this began the healing and balancing of her thyroid.

Weight Problems

Emotions

Angels say that emotions are held in your solar plexus, in the stomach area. This is the area of your inner power and control. Those who have a healthy, balanced control mechanism are able to maintain their weight, positive beliefs and expectations. Those consumed by negative feelings such as guilt, anger and low confidence will have a problem with weight fluctuations. Many people try everything to lose weight and, even if they do succeed, may regain it. Looking at the difficulty in terms of energy, the person may suffer from underlying negative beliefs or programming. It is these which need to be addressed and reprogrammed in order to prevent undesired changes in weight. It is the throat chakra that controls the thyroid function, the hormone which balances the metabolism. When you do not release your emotions through the throat chakra, it becomes damaged and clogged up, having a negative impact on the balance of your metabolism. When you begin to communicate and release all destructive energies from within your body, the throat and solar plexus chakras will work together to regulate and help you maintain your ideal weight.

Ideal Weight

It is important to know what your ideal weight is, to focus on being at this weight and to really believe that you can achieve and maintain it. If you cannot visualize yourself at your ideal or pre-ferred weight and your focus is on struggling to achieve it, this is what you will attract more of – struggles. Your mind will be out of kilter, with your subconscious mind unable to direct you to what is good for you and accepting any belief you have as reality, until you choose to replace them. When you begin to focus on your desired weight and believe that you are already there, your Angels will start shifting your behaviour to that end, and guide you to remove certain eating habits and certain foods from your diet, and will also be working on balancing your chakras and healing your angelic body. All that you are on the outside is a reflection of all that is going on within you. Therefore, the simple rule of chang-ing your inner world applies when you are trying to lose weight.

Anger

When you feel angry, your natural instincts are to want to punish someone or something. If you know who or what is making you angry, you have a few options. One is to confront, the other is to punish, and the other is to hold the anger within you. It may not be possible, or you may find it difficult to confront or punish someone, therefore, more than likely you will suppress it and try to move on. Anger is a very negative, low-energy frequency, and it does not disappear when it is ignored; it is just covered up.

The home of all fear-based emotions is your stomach area, which is governed by the solar plexus chakra, the area of your inner power. The only way to cover up these emotions is by comfort eating, and by doing this, you are literally feeding your anger. This becomes a habit, and your subconscious mind comes to believe that it is a healthy way of controlling your negative emotions. Unfortunately, then this becomes programmed into your subconscious mind, and a pattern is created which you will find difficult to break, unless you become aware that you are actually suppressing anger by eating. You may be exercising, eating healthy foods, dieting and consciously trying to lose weight, however, until you confront the anger stored within you, you will continue to subconsciously punish yourself in destructive ways.

Angel Healing helps you to find and release the anger and programmes of behaviour that are deeply ingrained in your subconscious mind in order to free you from the inner misery that is building up within you. The Angels provide a safe way for you to let the energy out without feeling the need to punish yourself or those you believe have caused the anger. Anger subsumes your cells with irritation and spreads through your body like fire. Angel Starlight energy puts out this fire with its gentle, cooling light. If you are not consciously aware of the reason for your anger, through a deep meditation the Angels can bring this to your attention and release it, no matter when or why it was originally created.

Emptiness

You may be feeling neglected by those you love, by your soul or your Creator. On a deeper level, you may feel a void which you are desperately trying somehow to fill. Comfort or excessive eating is one of the self-destructive methods you may be using to rid yourself of this feeling of emptiness. The emotion this causes in the long run is guilt. You may feel guilty, firstly, for eating more than you actually need and, secondly, for not looking after your body. This emotion also stays suppressed within you, or constantly gets covered up or denied. The Angels want to help you to fill your void with self-love and to transmute the energy of guilt into peace. They also want to remind you that everything you seek is actually within yourself. There is no void, and emptiness is an illusion, often caused by comparing your life to another person's life or to what society expects you to have achieved.

Protection

Excess weight is a form of protection which you have subconsciously created. It is important to find out why you feel the need to be protected, and when this began. The Angels will guide you to remember the past experiences that have caused you to want protection. People who are overweight from a very young age are actually very sensitive, and feel they need to be protected spiritually in this world. As they grow older, they may be bullied because of their weight, therefore they begin to feel a need for emotional protection. These people grow up feeling anger and resentment towards others, and as if they have to try harder to belong. As a consequence, they may have many insecurities and imbalances of confidence. Angel Healing allows you to go back in time and to transmute all the negative memories and patterns, and the need for protection, by transmuting the energy into positivity and breaking the patterns within the subconscious mind. This will then be reflected into the physical body and into your life as your confidence begins to grow.

ANGEL HEALING MEDITATION FOR WEIGHT PROBLEMS

ANGEL SECRET:

*'A stubborn mind creates stubborn weight;
excess emotion means excess weight.'*

CROWN CHAKRA

Angel Starlight enters your angelic body through a beautiful white rose just above your physical body. You see a silvery

sparkling star in the centre of your crown chakra and connect with your soul. Your Guardian Angel now guides you to access your negative beliefs about your weight. As they come into your consciousness, think more deeply until you find the negative programme relating to weight loss. This may be 'Losing weight is impossible' or 'Excess weight runs in the family.' When you find the negative programme, or programmes, see that the Angel Starlight energy filters all the way through to the core and transmutes it or them into a positive statement, such as 'Achieving and maintaining my perfect weight is effortless.'

THIRD-EYE CHAKRA

Angel Starlight travels down into the purple rose between your two eyes and into your mind. It now begins to clear your intuition blocks. Your Guardian Angel now opens your intuitive third eye, and you begin to scan your emotional body to find where all the negative emotions are being held within your physical body. As you intuitively scan your angelic body, visualize the Angel Starlight breaking up the emotions into small particles in the areas within your physical body which they have clogged up. As they dissolve, you can visualize your excess weight dropping off. The Angel Starlight now seals your physical body so that the excess weight will never build up again.

THROAT CHAKRA

Angel Starlight travels down into the blue rose in your throat and extends towards your ears. Your Guardian Angel now asks you to look deep within this chakra and to access all that is blocked and which you have not been able to communicate. You begin to speak, and release everything held within this area. Even if it makes no sense to you, just allow the suppressed feelings to be communicated. When everything is released, visualize your thyroid gland, which is in the physical part of your throat chakra within your body. Notice how dark and weak it has become over the years in which you have suppressed your emotions. Visualize the golden Angel Starlight running through and energizing this gland as it begins to function properly. Then visualize a beautiful stream of chemicals being released, which look like pure water drops coming from your thyroid gland and running through your whole body, regulating your metabolism.

HEART CHAKRA

Angel Starlight travels down into the green rose within your heart and, as it blossoms, you see that it slowly transforms into a pink rose. Your Guardian Angel now asks you to look within your heart and feel whether there is a feeling of emptiness. Visualize Angel Starlight filling this emptiness in your heart with the Angels' unconditional love. Feel inspired to achieve your weight-loss goals and believe with all your heart that you are supported rather than judged by the Angels along this journey.

SOLAR PLEXUS CHAKRA

Angel Starlight travels down into the yellow rose within your stomach area, the core of your being. Your Guardian Angel brings to the surface all your feelings of anger. Before you can feel the burning, irritating feelings of anger themselves, feel them being pulled out of your physical body by your Guardian Angel and washed away by the golden, cooling light. Visualize that every dark, negative cord attaching you to the people, places or situations that caused you anger is being cut by Archangel Michael, using his powerful sword. Feel Archangel Raphael's green healing energy now being channelled into your stomach and through your solar plexus and dissolving all traces of anger. Thank these Archangels for their healing energies.

SACRAL CHAKRA

Angel Starlight travels down into the orange rose just below your navel and activates your creative abilities. Your Guardian Angel brings your awareness to any guilt that you may be holding within your body. List everything you feel guilty about, without going into much detail, and see these issues individually being taken away by your Guardian Angel and transmuted into innocence, before being placed back into your sacral chakra. The energy of innocence releases all the attachments that are holding you in guilt, and you can use it as creative energy, to channel into something much more beneficial. Ask your Guardian Angel to let the feeling of forgiveness run within you, and as you forgive yourself, visualize that everyone you may need forgiveness from is forgiving you on a soul level now.

ROOT CHAKRA

Angel Starlight travels down into the red rose at the base of your spine. Your Guardian Angel asks you to visualize yourself at your ideal weight, looking and feeling wonderful about yourself. Feel excited about your new health and fitness regime, as your Guardian Angel now motivates you to create a new way of living, from this moment onwards. Feel that your relationship with food is now very healthy, and the relationship between your body, mind, heart and soul is very positive and balanced. Repeat the affirmation: 'I am my perfect, ideal weight.'

Success Story

Gaby had Angel Healing in order to deal with her weight problems. In the course of her meditation, the Angels showed me that she had been harbouring anger within her body and that she felt the need to be protected and was therefore intentionally gaining weight in order to feel physically and emotionally stronger. The healing energy would begin flowing through her body but would become stuck in her stomach area. Her solar plexus chakra had become dark and small instead of being a bright golden colour exuding the energy of power, stability and confidence. When I asked Gaby how she felt, she replied, 'Very nauseous and hot.' I guided her to access the negative emotions that had been building up within her and regressed her into the past. Immediately she became aware that she had been holding in her anger since a traumatic experience at work about three years previously which had set her off into a spiralling depression. She had been physically attacked by a customer and had also been emotionally bullied by her manager for years and told not to take any action against the attacker but to forget about it. This had completely ruined her confidence and self-esteem. The Angels explained that this had been a pattern that had repeated itself in her life since childhood – she felt inadequate and under attack. After releasing these negative emotions, patterns and memories, Gaby regained her inner power. I asked her to visualize herself as an attractive person who was now able to be in control of her life and of her eating patterns. Almost immediately, she changed her lifestyle, and started losing weight.

Attractiveness

Appearance

When you begin to channel the energy of Angels, many changes happen to your appearance, both visibly and in terms of energy. The energy field around your physical body becomes a lot brighter and more attractive to others, even if they cannot physically see any changes. The Angel Starlight energy works from the inside and reflects out through your eyes, and you are able to see the world from a pure perspective with love. Your Guardian Angel usually stands behind you, ready to wrap their wings around you when you need to be protected. To have a natural, attractive glow, ask your Guardian Angel to step closer into your body and channel their golden light through you. This is very healing for you, as it transmutes all the negative energy and darkness within your angelic body into positive energy and light, and in so doing makes you very attractive.

Smile

Angels say that a person's face is a reflection of their heart and that smiling is the expression of the heart's loving emotions. When the Angels open your heart to love, the vibration of love goes into each cell and organ of your physical body. Your smile is the biggest asset you possess in attracting others, and making an impression. Smiling reduces stress levels and releases the happy hormones. When you smile at another person, it automatically uplifts them. When you smile at a person, you prompt a heart-to-heart connection, and you help them to acknowledge their qualities of kindness. A smile does not cost you anything; however, it can go a very long way, as the universe reacts towards you with love, bringing you many fantastic opportunities – as well as freebies and good deals on purchases! A smile is a very effective way to spread the Angel's love, and your rewards from the angelic realm are magnificent.

Grace

Angels carry the energy of grace. When you connect with and channel the Angels, you begin to exude a gentle energy of elegance. Real, natural beauty is long-lasting and will make an unforgettable impression upon others. Allowing your natural, loving and kind personality to shine through immediately makes you attractive to others. When you walk with grace, shining the light of the Angels through your eyes and expressing the love within your heart by smiling, you remove all pretence. It is when you live as your authentic, beautiful self that you are more likely to attract people's attention, and you will be known for your angelic integrity and have a reputation as a beautiful person.

Energy

Attractiveness does not come just from within. When you are accepted by others in society, you feel a sense of belonging, therefore you don't erect so many barriers against interacting with others. It is important to have or work towards having high levels of self-esteem, self-acceptance and self-respect. Once this is attained, and depending on your values and priorities, it is your presentation of yourself that transmits energy to the world you live in, and the world will transmit the same quality of energy back into your life. The Angels know and tell us that being beautiful on the inside is definitely the most permanent and inexpensive way of being beautiful on the outside.

Style

Having a unique style of appearance and character is an expression of your creative energy. It also sends out messages that you are confident, and confidence is one of the most attractive qualities you can possess. Setting a trend which will inspire others in a positive way is very empowering and can lead to respect from others. Angels will help you to find your unique style and express this through your dress sense, the interior design of your home or through the way in which you approach your work. As your inner world reflects your outer world, the outer world reflects your inner world. When you look good, you feel good; and when you feel good, you look good.

ANGEL HEALING MEDITATION FOR ATTRACTIVENESS

ANGEL SECRET:

'The sacred beauty of your soul shines through your eyes.'

CROWN CHAKRA

Angel Starlight enters your angelic body through a beautiful white rose just above your physical body. You see a silvery sparkling star in the centre of your crown chakra and connect with your soul. Your Guardian Angel now guides you to find and connect with your inner beauty.

THIRD-EYE CHAKRA

Angel Starlight travels down into the purple rose between your two eyes and into your mind. It now begins to clear your intuition blocks. Your Guardian Angel guides you into a golden sacred temple where you take a seat on a throne. The beauty of your soul now shines though your eyes to fill the temple with bright sparkling white light.

THROAT CHAKRA

Angel Starlight travels down into the blue rose in your throat and extends towards your ears. Your Guardian Angel now asks you to repeat the words, 'I now shine the beauty of my soul into my life.' Visualize this healing light extending out into the world, connecting with the inner beauty of others' souls. As each person is touched by the beauty of your soul, they each awaken to the love of their Guardian Angels.

HEART CHAKRA

Angel Starlight travels down into the green rose within your heart and, as it blossoms, you see that it slowly transforms into a pink rose. Your Guardian Angel now thanks you for the kindness that you show to the world with your beauty and places eternal love into your heart. You now find it in your heart to forgive those who have not seen or appreciated your inner beauty in the past and the eternal love from your Guardian Angel.

SOLAR PLEXUS CHAKRA

Angel Starlight travels down into the yellow rose within your stomach area, the core of your being. Your Guardian Angel now straightens and elongates your spine, which at the same time completely aligns your chakras. Visualize and feel this improving your posture and releasing the heaviness from your shoulders.

SACRAL CHAKRA

Angel Starlight travels down into the orange rose just below your navel and activates your creative abilities. Your Guardian Angel brings your awareness to your sexuality and transmutes all negative beliefs about your power, status and gender into positive ones. Feel your sacral chakra being cleansed of all guilt or shame and visualize the beautiful orange rose blossoming and glowing within your body, ready to connect through a loving relationship and experience the power of sacred love as pleasure.

ROOT CHAKRA

Angel Starlight travels down into the red rose at the base of your spine. Your Guardian Angel guides you back out of the golden temple and into your body. You are now feeling youthful and looking radiant. The joy of your heart is shining through your smile and the beauty of your soul is shining through your eyes. Every person you come into contact with will notice your natural attractiveness and will feel drawn to your infectious energy. As you spread the beauty of your soul into the Universe, you communicate with others on a soul level rather than on an ego level, therefore awakening the beauty within them too.

Success Story

As a child, like many people, I compared myself to others and felt that I was not good-looking or attractive enough. I suffered skin problems for years, which made me feel even worse about myself. When I found out about Angel Healing, I asked the Angels to help me feel comfortable in my own skin. My Guardian Angel showed me that my inner irritations and low self-esteem were manifesting themselves in my external body. During my meditations, I would feel the healing light going into every cell of my body and cleansing my skin as well as putting the fire out from under my skin. I began to feel natural again, and no longer felt the need to use layers of make-up and cover up my true identity. As time went by, I started to treat myself better, and look after my skin. The skin irritations cleared up naturally and, in time, the scars faded away too. I also found that, during certain phases of depression, I was prone to accidents and would burn my skin by accident. Through Angel Healing, I learned that this was a way of punishing myself and demonstrating that I didn't love myself.

Lethargy

Tiredness

Angels realize that people never feel that there is enough time to complete all their daily chores and fulfil all their responsibilities, let alone to spend quality time with those who deserve your attention. People end up burning out and feeling lethargic, which leads to ill health. Life on Earth is moving at such a fast pace, and people are trying to keep up with all that is happening. Moments of relaxation or holidays should not be seen as luxuries, they should be a vital part of life and should not make you feel guilty. Angels can bring back into your life your natural liveliness so that you can enjoy each moment. They will guide you towards being playful, energetic and an inspiration to others by radiating a positive attitude as well as vibes of happiness which will uplift others.

Low Energy

One of the quickest ways to boost your energy is by taking regular five-minute Angel Healing breaks, wherever you happen to be. By closing your eyes and bringing your attention to your inner state of being you will be able to control your heart rate, still the rate of mental activity and rest your body as you reconnect with your soul. A longer twenty- to thirty-minute meditation each day will boost your energy levels naturally, as you remove dense energy from your energy field which weighs your body down.

Being inactive also lowers energy levels, therefore the Angels will guide you to a more active, yet balanced lifestyle. Walks in nature are very healing for the body, mind, heart and soul, as you can connect with the Nature Angels and talk to them about everything that is weighing you down in life.

Exhaustion

Angels realize that people cram so much into everyday life that they suffer stress if they feel unable to achieve their goals, and this leaves them feeling mentally and physically exhausted. This is detrimental towards your health and well-being and will cause the body to shut down when it can no longer cope with the pressures placed upon it. It also has a negative impact on emotions, and you may be left feeling frustrated or angry. On a mental level, exhaustion may take away clarity and motivation, and you may lose focus on achieving happiness on all levels. Angel Healing techniques such as meditation, relaxation and deep-breathing exercises all contribute to healing exhaustion and increasing physical energy levels. Angels will help you to assess the amount of tasks you are taking on each day and help you to delegate, eliminate and prioritize accordingly. The Angels will also guide you towards changing your eating habits and will encourage you to drink more water, which is very cleansing and energizing, as it removes the toxins within you.

Feeling Drained

If certain people, places or situations drain your energy, it is because they are surrounded by dark negativity and, on the level of energy, they are taking your light and positive energy. Although many people do not consciously set out to drain happiness or peace from you, on a soul level they are crying out for healing. Energetically, we form invisible but strong cords or bonds between ourselves and anything we come into contact with. Attachments form between you and other people, places, work, home, situations or countries, and when these attachments are healthy, the pure energy of love flows through, bringing you happiness. However, when any of these attachments become unhealthy, negative energy starts running through these cords and makes its way into your angelic body. The Angels bring your attention to negative attachments or patterns in your life in your intuition and meditation sessions. They are able to vacuum the negativity poured into your angelic body from external sources and will then fill you with pure Angel Starlight energy to purify all traces of darkness before strengthening and protecting you from similar situations in the future.

ANGEL HEALING MEDITATION FOR LETHARGY

ANGEL SECRET:

*'When you are too tired,
it means you have tried too hard.'*

CROWN CHAKRA

Angel Starlight enters your angelic body through a beautiful white rose just above your physical body. You see a silvery sparkling star in the centre of your crown chakra and connect with your soul. Your Guardian Angel now guides you to breathe the energizing Angel Starlight deeply into your mind then completely release all thoughts as you breathe out. Repeat this three times.

THIRD-EYE CHAKRA

Angel Starlight travels down into the purple rose between your two eyes and into your mind. It now begins to clear your intuition blocks. Your Guardian Angel now carries your tired body into a beautiful paradise where there is a white sandy beach, a clear blue sky and a big beautiful hammock for you to lounge in between two palm trees. As you lie down, swinging gently and gazing up into the sky, you feel the sun beaming down into your body and re-energizing you.

THROAT CHAKRA

Angel Starlight travels down into the blue rose in your throat and extends towards your ears. As your Guardian Angel takes a step back to leave you with your thoughts, you fall into a deeper state of relaxation, letting your entire body relax for a few more moments. Repeat the affirmation: 'I am completely relaxed.'

HEART CHAKRA

Angel Starlight travels down into the green rose within your heart and, as it blossoms, you see that it slowly transforms into a pink rose. Your Guardian Angel now brings forward two other healing Angels, one to stand either side of your body, which is still lying, beautifully relaxed, on the hammock. These Angels now send multicoloured healing energies into your body, which represent nourishment, rehydration and replenishment within your body. They also remove the tension from within your muscles and channel soothing balm into your tired body.

SOLAR PLEXUS CHAKRA

Angel Starlight travels down into the yellow rose within your stomach area, the core of your being. Thank the two Angels for their healing as they prepare to leave. Use your intuition to look within and around your angelic body to locate any negative cords attaching you to people or situations which may be draining your energy each day. Visualize the golden Angel Starlight dissolving all negative attachments for your highest and best good, and that these are never to be attached to you again without your will.

SACRAL CHAKRA

Angel Starlight travels down into the orange rose just below your navel and activates your creative abilities. Speak to your Guardian Angel now about the changes you will be making to your daily routine in order to reduce the symptoms of lethargy and fatigue, and to boost your energy levels. Your Guardian Angel will ensure that you break the destructive patterns that have become embedded in your day and will impart to you many short cuts, delegation techniques and organizational skills.

ROOT CHAKRA

Angel Starlight travels down into the red rose at the base of your spine. Your Guardian Angel now carries you from your hammock through the beautiful, relaxing paradise, back into your body, where you continue to keep the feeling of serenity with you throughout your whole day and every other day. When you feel exhausted and that you need a holiday, you will always be able to retreat back into this paradise with your Guardian Angel.

Success Story

Elaine had Angel Healing for Chronic Fatigue Syndrome. During her meditation, the Angels showed me that she felt tired of giving so much of herself to others and not feeling appreciated. This resonated with Elaine, and she began to explain that, in her career, she had been a high-flyer, working as a personal assistant to the director of a law firm. Eventually, she had become so physically exhausted that her body shut down. As the healing energy started to flow through her, it became apparent that her life-force energy was extremely low, her energy chakras had become blocked, and she was consumed with the fear of facing everyday life, as she had no more energy to give. As Archangel Raphael transformed her negative energy, she began to feel hope again and found it easier to pursue her interests in personal development in order to get her life back on track and to beat the symptoms of CFS.

Sleep and Astral Travel

Space and Time

As I have mentioned before, Angels exist in a different dimension to us, therefore they are not restricted by space or time. The loving and healing energy of the Angels can be directed across time, going backwards through the ancestral line to heal members of your family, healing in your present moment, or going forward into future lifetimes. Their love for you is constant and, of course, there is your one special Guardian Angel who will stay with you throughout all time and knows everything about your destiny. As you raise the frequency of your energy and expand your consciousness, you become aware of the Angels' presence with you on Earth. There is only a thin veil separating the different realms, so the Angels can float between the angelic and Earth realms easily. They can also bring things into your physical life much more quickly than your limited conscious mind may imagine, as they are able to manipulate energy.

Astral Travel

If you have had the experience of your consciousness leaving your physical body for a short amount of time, you have experienced astral travel (otherwise known as an out-of-body experience) between different realms of existence. Your Guardian Angel will ensure that a silver cord is attached to your physical body and that you will return fully into your body after your travels.

With your eyes closed, your senses are much sharper and your vision is more creative, therefore, it may seem as if you are actually living that moment in your reality. There are no physical limitations when you are astral travelling, so speed, time and space do not exist. You can go back in time or fast-forward into your future. You can astral travel during meditations, or while you are sleeping – or even daydreaming. All that is required is that you focus on your intention of travelling beyond your physical dimension. During Angel Healing, astral travel can be used to perform distant healing for others, to find lost items, to connect with other souls and to visit the angelic realm. There are many levels within the angelic realm which you can explore and learn from.

Actual Travel

When you are travelling with your physical body, the Angels will protect you from any harmful accidents when you call upon them. By asking the Angels to send Angel Starlight energy into your entire journey, they will find ways to overcome all obstacles and prevent accidents. Archangel Raphael is the Angel of Travel, and he will oversee all your travels, looking after you, your family, your luggage and the vehicles you travel on. If you get lost on your journey, this Angel will whisper guidance into your mind so that you can take the appropriate action to find your way back on to your path. Miracles such as petrol being topped up, or people appearing when the car has broken down somewhere off the beaten track, is always the loving service of the Angels. When you hear of or see any accidents, ask the Angels to kindly send healing energy to all those involved and to comfort any injured people. You can ask your Guardian Angel to make your journey as smooth as possible for you, and to keep you calm and safe.

Commuting

There is a huge build-up of negative and dense energy on many public-transport systems, most especially when travelling underground. This negativity consists of the daily stress of millions of people each day and the traumatic passing of souls through accidents. The environment is not cleansed by fresh air flowing through it, so commuters are breathing stale energy into their bodies. Commuting during rush hours in busy cities is very tiring and draining; it can be exhausting and create a negative start to each day. The collective consciousness of stress, of rushing, of panic and anger at delays is absorbed by your subconscious mind and affects your mood before you even start work. As you become more sensitive to the subtle energies around you through Angel Healing, you may pick up on the negativity while you are commuting. If you call upon the Angels, they can help in many ways. Firstly, they will place a shield around your angelic body to protect you from absorbing the negative energy. Secondly, they will direct the Angel Starlight to cleanse and break down the accretion of negative energy. If Angels are called upon everyday by many people who commute, there will be an accumulation of healing light which will be directed into the darkness which is causing many city workers' energy to burn out. The Angels will transmute the stress of commuters into peace and calmness, and this will bring order into your journey. A byproduct of this will be that the problems endured by millions of people every day will be reduced.

Sleep

While you are asleep, your soul may visit different realms and link with other souls. You have the power to choose where you want to go before you fall asleep. One of the places your soul goes is the spiritual realm, in order to discuss your next step in life and ask how to deal with certain situations; here, you are given premonitions of the future. These premonitions are often referred to as psychic dreams, and when the incident occurs in the physical realm, there is a sense of déjà vu. If your mission in life involves teaching others, especially about spiritual matters, your soul goes to a spiritual school to be taught by high-level guides, so that you can pass on the wisdom to your students. As you practise Angel Healing on others as a practitioner or teacher, soul connections and cords are formed between you and your clients or students. During the state of sleep, you may carry out your healing for others by astral travelling in order to connect with them on a soul level. The reason why many people comment that they have dreamt about their spiritual practitioners and teachers is because of these spiritual connections.

Insomnia is usually caused by underlying fears keeping the mind active. By calling the Angels to your side before you fall asleep, they will guide you into a meditation which will help you to connect with the angelic energy, transform the stress or tension within your physical body and clear your mind to bring you a restful sleep. Placing a piece of rose quartz crystal under your pillow will protect you from lower energies and will keep the Angels around you while you sleep.

ANGEL HEALING MEDITATION FOR TRAVEL

ANGEL SECRET:

'Your consciousness follows your intentions.'

CROWN CHAKRA

Angel Starlight enters your angelic body through a beautiful white rose just above your physical body. You see a silvery sparkling star in the centre of your crown chakra and connect with your soul. As you prepare to go on an astral journey, your Guardian Angel places a protective layer of the golden Angel Starlight energy around your angelic body. Visualize that you are leaving your physical body, a silver cord attached between your physical and your angelic body. You begin to float upwards with your Guardian Angel by your side. As you ascend higher, look down at the Earth's natural beauty. Before completely leaving the Earth realm, you sense all the energy that has built up within the Earth's body of energy, which surround the planet in much the same way as your aura surrounds your physical body. Communicate with the Earth from a higher level to understand what it is crying out for and how you can contribute to making the world a better place to live in. Visualize what this energy looks like in colour, density, vitality and try to discern whether it is causing the Earth any distress.

THIRD-EYE CHAKRA

Angel Starlight travels down into the purple rose between your two eyes and into your mind. It now begins to clear your intuition blocks. You now enter the first layer of the beautiful angelic realm. This is the home of the Guardian Angels and many other Angels – those who are the closest to humanity. These Angels come from all the different categories, such as Angels of Wisdom, Intuition, Communication, Love, Power, Creativity and Security. All these Angels have the purpose of healing humanity by helping them with certain issues and transforming our lives. Spend time speaking to these Angels about your challenges or in order to learn from their divine knowledge. See that they always connect with you during your Angel Healing meditations to enhance the benefits that you receive. These lovely Angels will become your companions and will help you with anything you need at any time in your life, as long as your intentions are pure and as long as you feel gratitude for their help.

THROAT CHAKRA

Angel Starlight travels down into the blue rose in your throat and extends towards your ears. When you and your Guardian Angel are ready to move on, the bubble holding you both ascends higher and higher, passing many unusual, colourful lights in space. You are now entering the second layer of the angelic realm. This is the home of the Archangels, and you are greeted by the mighty Archangel Michael. He communicates with you regarding your courage and thanks you for being a channel of Angel Healing energy. He introduces you to the other Archangels and you spend time communicating with them individually. You now enter the third layer of the angelic realm. This is the home of the principalities, the Angels that oversee and help groups as a whole, such as organizations, cities and countries. Ask these Angels to send healing to our government, our financial systems, and to channel positive energy into countries where there is war. Thank these Angels for their help.

HEART CHAKRA

Angel Starlight travels down into the green rose within your heart and, as it blossoms, you see that it slowly transforms into a pink rose. You are now entering the fourth layer of the angelic realm. This is the home of the powers; these are known as the gatekeepers of all the records relating to humanity. The Angels of Birth, Death and Rebirth belong within this group. They protect all souls from negative forces and are also professors and educators. They hold the intelligence of astronomy and sacred geometry. You now enter the fifth layer of the angelic realm. This is the home of the virtues, the Angels of Miracles and Great Blessings. They are also referred to as the Brilliant and Shining Ones, as they channel enormous amounts of divine light into our world.

SOLAR PLEXUS CHAKRA

Angel Starlight travels down into the yellow rose within your stomach area, the core of your being. You are now entering the sixth level of the angelic realm. This is the home of the dominions, the Angels who are responsible for the teaching and development of all other Angels. You now enter the seventh level of the angelic realm. This is the home of the thrones, the Angels of Planets. These Angels support the Throne of God and decide how His decisions will be manifested. They are the judges of individual karma and the karma of different societies.

SACRAL CHAKRA

Angel Starlight travels down into the orange rose just below your navel and activates your creative abilities. You now enter the eighth level of the angelic realm. This is the home of the Cherubim, the Guardians of Light which emanates from the sun, moon and stars. They are some of the most powerful Angels, and are very close to God. Their responsibilities include maintaining the records of Heaven. You now enter the ninth level of the angelic realm. This is the home of the highest-ranking Angels, the Seraphim. They are the most evolved beings and the closest to God, as they surround his throne. They control the movement of the planets, stars and Heavens using sound.

ROOT CHAKRA

Angel Starlight travels down into the red rose at the base of your spine. Your Guardian Angel guides you back to the Earth realm now that you have explored all nine levels of the angelic realm. Before coming back into your body, you are able to visit any place in the world that you wish to. Take this opportunity to connect with the beautiful dolphins realm for serenity and peace, connect with the elemental fairies realm for playfulness and fun, or connect with the unicorns realm for their ancient wisdom. When you are ready, visualize and feel yourself coming into your physical body, fully grounding your energy as you bring your attention to your heartbeat and to your physical surroundings. Take a few long deep breaths in, and place you feet firmly on the ground as the excess energy flows into the Earth, creating the roots which will keep you grounded.

Success Story

Meera sought out Angel Healing because she was having difficulty sleeping. In the course of her meditation, the Angels told me that she had an extremely active mind and found it very difficult to switch off, especially at night, as she would lie awake thinking about any problems she was experiencing. The Angels asked her to carry out a simple visualization technique whereby, in her mind, she would see a circle divided into sections, each

representing a certain area of her life, such as home, relationships, finance and work. I asked her to place all her thoughts into
the appropriate sections, as if she was filing them away, but that
she could easily retrieve them the following day if she wanted to.
The Angels wanted her to feel that she was letting go and releasing any worrying thoughts or challenges into their hands, and as
the healing energy flowed through her mind, it removed all
unnecessary thoughts that were cluttering her mind. This made
Meera feel that she was in control, much more organized and as
if a weight had been lifted from her. Then, she was guided to
think about her bedroom and to picture herself trying to sleep.
As she was drifting into a deep meditation, I asked her to feel
whereabouts in her bedroom there was stagnant or dense energy
that was stopping her from sleeping properly. She described her
room as very cluttered, with clothes under her bed and bulging
wardrobes, and said that it needed a good clear-out – especially
those items which belonged to her ex-partner. After her healing
meditation, Meera felt inspired to organize her life and realized
that this had to begin with reorganizing her mind, her bedroom
and her living space. Archangel Gabriel was invoked to purify her
life, and Meera was given a meditation to follow every night
before sleeping. This has helped with her sleeping issues and she
has developed her meditation and healing abilities.

Depression

Giving Up

Depression eventually works its way into the physical body, causing it to give up fighting. This creates very low morale and leaves the sufferer with hardly any energy with which to face life. This disease destroys self-esteem and confidence, mainly because the sufferer is consumed with feelings of failure. Angels will restore the hope that he or she can overcome depression and renew their zest for life by opening their eyes to a higher perspective. Angels say that depression is often a cry for 'time out' and reflection 'with-in'.

Suppression

Depression comes from something within you being suppressed rather than expressed. As the body is closely linked with the mind, heart and soul, depression can manifest itself on any level and in any way, and you may not even know why. Angel Healing will heal the cause of depression as well as the symptoms; this will prevent it from recurring. During meditation, you go inwards and connect with your emotions and thoughts. You can then look deeper within yourself to see what it is that is creating certain emotions and thoughts by using your intuition and the guidance of your Guardian Angel.

Purpose

As with all challenges that face us, depression has a higher purpose. It provides an opportunity for your current life patterns to come to a halt. It opens out a way of rebuilding your life when it has collapsed, and rebuilding it in such a way that it serves you, rather than the way you have been taught or told to live it by a source external to you. Depression brings about a transition. Everything goes through cycles of endings and beginnings in life; if this didn't happen, there would be no change towards achieving true happiness. Angels know that when you are faced with voluntary or involuntary transitional periods in your life, you feel ungrounded and insecure. Fear creeps in and wants to remove your power and control. This creates havoc within your body and it becomes too much for you to handle. The Angels want to teach you how to embrace change. They will reassure you and show you the good that is to come from the change that is about to happen in your life. They no longer want to see you living a life in which you are not fulfilled; they want you to use your highest potential and creativity. Angels will wrap you in their wings and comfort you and gently carry you forward to the next phase of your life. Make space for your new life by cutting away the negative attachments to the old and outdated. Give thanks and gratitude for what was and look forward with excitement to what will be.

No Energy

When your life-force energy flows through your angelic body with no interference or blockages, this creates vitality and well-being. If the energy is unable to flow and gets stuck within a chakra or an area in your angelic body, energy begins to build up, which will eventually affect your mental and emotional bodies. This leads to your physical body feeling heavy, which will slow you down. It also leads to frustration within the mind and the bloating of emotions, building up ready to explode at any moment. Angels will channel the Angel Starlight energy through all of your chakras and through your entire body to release these build-ups. They will especially concentrate on your throat chakra, to allow you to express clearly how you are feeling. Even if it makes no sense to you at the time, it will be a very good release of the stale energy which is blocking the flow of life-force energy. After Angel Healing, you may feel teary, but this is actually a good sign. Crying is also a form of releasing energy, especially emotions, and once these are out of your system, there will be new space for you to fill up with happiness and joy.

ANGEL HEALING MEDITATION FOR DEPRESSION

ANGEL SECRET:

'Suppression causes depression; release brings relief.'

CROWN CHAKRA

Angel Starlight enters your angelic body through a beautiful white rose just above your physical body. You may feel it takes a little longer to open your crown chakra and receive the healing energy. Your Guardian Angel patiently waits by your side until you are ready to heal your depression. You see a silvery sparkling star in the centre of your crown chakra and connect with your soul.

THIRD-EYE CHAKRA

Angel Starlight travels down into the purple rose between your two eyes and into your mind. It now begins to clear your intuition blocks. Your Guardian Angel opens your third eye so that you can intuitively see into your body. Notice the effects that your mood has had on your angelic body. What can you see when you look within? Depression often causes darkness and frailness, and works to close up your chakras, therefore life-force energy is unable to flow freely and give you vitality. Visualize the Angel Starlight energy going into these areas and adjusting your energetic body back to its normal state.

THROAT CHAKRA

Angel Starlight travels down into the blue rose in your throat and extends towards your ears. Your Guardian Angel now asks you to think about what you are suppressing. Choose to speak out loud or in your mind about what form of energy you are not letting out and why. When you identify this energy, ask your Guardian Angel to intervene and help you to release the thoughts and emotions causing you depression. Your Guardian Angel will now reassure you that they have been released and you will be comforted by their understanding, compassion and love.

HEART CHAKRA

Angel Starlight travels down into the green rose within your heart and, as it blossoms, you see that it slowly transforms into a pink rose. Your Guardian Angel now connects deeply with your heart and reawakens your joy for life. Visualize joy as a multicoloured light running from your heart into all other areas of your body, clearing all blocks and allowing your life-force energy to continue running effortlessly through your body. As this is happening, visualize and feel that a beautiful chemical is being produced from your brain. This chemical is serotonin; it looks like trickles of tiny pure water drops going into each cell, tissue and organ within your body.

SOLAR PLEXUS CHAKRA

Angel Starlight travels down into the yellow rose within your stomach area, the core of your being. Your Guardian Angel asks you to take three long, deep breaths in and out, and you relax further as you absorb the energies of joy and happiness from the serotonin. Once you have done this, feel that negative feelings such as loneliness, worthlessness, sadness and jealousy are all being transmuted by the golden Angel Starlight into strength and confidence. Your Guardian Angel reconnects you with your true spiritual self, who is peace, love and joy.

SACRAL CHAKRA

Angel Starlight travels down into the orange rose just below your navel and activates your creative abilities. Your Guardian Angel reminds you that you are in control of your life, including your feelings, moods, actions and thoughts. All bitterness or blame is now dissolved as you remember all the good things that you can create in your life. Visualize what you would like to have in your life now in order to stop depression from returning. Begin an action plan in your mind and use your natural creative abilities along with Angel Healing to heal all blocks from achieving this reality.

ROOT CHAKRA

Angel Starlight travels down into the red rose at the base of your spine. Your Guardian Angel now brings your attention once more to your angelic body. As you scan all of your energetic bodies, channel extra golden Angel Starlight into vulnerable areas. Your Guardian Angel now places a protective layer around the edge of your angelic body to stop any external factors from causing any form of depression rising within you again. Feel ready to make a change in your outer world now that you feel better within yourself. You will see that your Guardian Angel has now removed all sorrow from your body and is carrying you forward to a better place.

Success Story

Angela suffered depression before, during and after her divorce. She was suffering from panic attacks and would cry all day. This was affecting her health, as she was unable to eat well or sleep properly. She was desperate to find the physical, emotional and mental strength to see her divorce through without allowing her estranged partner to take advantage of her. In her meditation, Angela was guided to the angelic realm for healing and rejuvenation. She was introduced to her Guardian Angel, who she could see, hear and feel very clearly. This connection empowered her on every level to feel that she did have the inner strength to get through the depression and to change her life for the better after many years of suffering. She saw her Guardian Angel working alongside her family members in the spirit world. This gave Angela the faith to stand her ground, knowing that she was supported by her Angels. Within days, she began the divorce proceedings against her abusive, unfaithful husband. Her emotions were a lot more under control, and she knew she could always turn to her Angels for guidance and healing along the way, trusting that they were on her side. She started eating better and was also able gradually to decrease and then stop taking medication for her depression.

Sensuality

Tantric Union

Tantra is a technique that is used to explore sensuality. It enhances self-transformation through complete self-awareness, which then creates a sense of liberation. The purpose of combining Tantra with Angel Healing is to unite the body, mind, heart and soul. It is the art of appreciating all senses in order to connect beyond the physical realm. It intensifies the pleasure you feel towards life on all levels of your being. Through your sensuality, you will discover bliss, and you will honour your physical body for all that it provides for you. In relationships, the merging of two bodies is actually the merging of souls. Angels want to heighten your sensitivity so that you can enjoy the many joys in your life, because you deserve to. Give all your inhibitions to the Angels so that you can enjoy fully expressing your divine femininity or masculinity without feeling self-conscious. This will lead to increased confidence, happiness and self-esteem as you start to believe that such joys are possible, and that you worthy of experiencing them. Connecting to another person through their eyes, the windows to their soul, deepens the understanding and love between you, as it leads you to look beyond the exterior. The passion between two souls ignites their life-force energy, which runs throughout the angelic body, increasing health and vitality, as well as releasing all the hormones which create balance and happiness. Best of all, this process will transmit pheromones, which make you very attractive to your partner in many ways.

Sacred Union

When two souls get together, they communicate in their own language: one of divine love. Words, thoughts and actions no longer have the power to control the outcome of this sacred union. It is a moment in your lifetime when you know that what is happening is not a chance meeting with a particular person, it is without a doubt written in the stars and meant to be. No matter how long you stay connected in a physical sense, after a sacred union, your soul cannot and doesn't ever forget. A sacred union with a member of your soul family or soul mate will bring you the highest form of pure love, and you will care for that person in every way; however, a sacred union with the other half of your soul, known as your twin soul, will knock you off your feet and blow you away!

The purpose of this meeting is not the formation of a romantic, lasting marriage but the higher hidden purpose of serving humanity by awakening the two individuals to their sacred missions in this particular lifetime. The Angels play a huge role in reuniting these two souls and helping them through the journey of separation when the time comes for each to continue independently along their own paths. The pain of separation can be as severe as grief and bereavement, however, each person will find solace in their work of fulfilling their life purpose.

The immense love between these souls can be destructive, and can have the power to completely demolish the structure of your life until that point. This is another important reason for sacred unions: so that you can rebuild your life in line with your true life path. Angels weep when they see the distress caused after a sacred union, however, they will ensure that both individuals are rewarded in the most beautiful way.

Blocks

Angels are able to help you release any blocks within your subconscious mind regarding your sexuality. These blocks may have been instilled at an early age, for example, you may have been told that intimacy is wrong, or that you will be taken advantage of or judged if you express your sexuality freely. No matter where the negative blocks or fears originate from, the Angels will remove them and leave only positive feelings, guiding you towards healthy liberation. By clearing the blocks within your mind, your new positive thoughts will be reflected in your emotions, and your emotions will be expressed through your actions. Angel Healing gives you the opportunity for new beginnings and a new lease of life, no matter what your previous experiences were. You will also find the balance between your feminine and masculine qualities, and this will shine through and draw an equally balanced and contented partner into your life.

ANGEL HEALING MEDITATION FOR SENSUALITY

ANGEL SECRET:

'Sensitivity creates sensuality;
sensuality expresses sexuality.'

CROWN CHAKRA

Angel Starlight enters your angelic body through a beautiful white rose just above your physical body. You see a silvery sparkling star in the centre of your crown chakra and connect with your soul. Your Guardian Angel now guides you to expand your consciousness way beyond the physical realms. Open your mind to a new way of experiencing the pleasures of life and visualize the Angel Starlight energy running through your nervous system, cleansing and enhancing your sensitivity in the best way.

THIRD-EYE CHAKRA

Angel Starlight travels down into the purple rose between your two eyes and into your mind. It now begins to clear your intuition blocks. Your Guardian Angel now shows you that all your five senses of touch, taste, smell, hearing and sight are purified with Angel Starlight energy. View yourself as a sensual person now, able to feel and express pleasure on all levels of your being.

THROAT CHAKRA

Angel Starlight travels down into the blue rose in your throat and extends towards your ears. Your Guardian Angel now asks you connect with your sexuality and speak about your blocks in expressing your sexuality effectively. Speak about your beliefs regarding your sexuality and what may be blocking or restricting you from expressing yourself. Speak about how your sexuality has been portrayed by your culture and society and give all the negativity to your Guardian Angel so that it can be changed into empowerment. Also hand over any fears of being misjudged by others to your Guardian Angel.

HEART CHAKRA

Angel Starlight travels down into the green rose within your heart and, as it blossoms, you see that it slowly transforms into a pink rose. Your Guardian Angel now asks you to feel both the feminine and masculine energies within your heart to be completely balanced. From your heart, send out into the universe a message that you are ready to experience a sacred union with your twin soul or soul mate. Visualize a stream of pink energy shining out of your heart chakra, magnetizing all experiences of great pleasure back into your life.

SOLAR PLEXUS CHAKRA

Angel Starlight travels down into the yellow rose within your stomach area, the core of your being. Your Guardian Angel now empowers you to feel absolutely beautiful and comfortable in your own skin. The divine feminine and masculine power is now coming from above, healing any blocks around, using your sensuality, charm and attractiveness in a powerful way.

SACRAL CHAKRA

Angel Starlight travels down into the orange rose just below your navel and activates your creative abilities. Your Guardian Angel sends more Angel Starlight into your reproductive area to transmute any negative memories, fears or traumas held within this area. Using your creative imagination, visualize yourself looking, feeling and being naturally sexy. Visualize yourself expressing your sensuality and femininity or masculinity through dance, art, drama or in any other creative way.

ROOT CHAKRA

Angel Starlight travels down into the red rose at the base of your spine. Your Guardian Angel now brings your awareness to your physical body. As you intuitively scan all your chakras, direct more Angel Starlight into the darker areas, which need healing, so that all tensions can be released. Visualize all your chakras glowing in different colours and sending out sacred feminine or masculine vibes in order to attract a sacred union with your twin soul. As you begin to see a sparkling star coming closer towards you, you realize that you are about to connect with your twin soul on a higher level. Visualize that this star is now merging with your soul, the star within your crown chakra. This merging illuminates your entire angelic body and reawakens your heart to your sacred mission here on Earth. Enjoy this state of bliss, and when the soul is ready to leave, send gratitude and blessings until you meet again.

Success Story

Sam came to Angel Healing to overcome his feeling of low self-esteem after several failed relationships. He thought he'd never find love, especially as he had no love for himself. He connected with the Angels by attending Angel Healing workshops and in them felt that Archangel Chamuel was all around him, surrounding him with little love cherubs! For his meditation, I channelled advice for him from his Guardian Angel, Archangel Chamuel and the love angels. He was told that the first step in finding true love was to reconnect to his true self. I delivered a message that he was to attend Tantra classes, and he was amazed that I mentioned this, as he had been receiving signs, messages and even invitations to explore Tantra for a while. He went home feeling great and inspired, and the next day he booked a private Tantric class, which he found very liberating. He went on to book a weekend Tantric retreat course, where he connected with someone on a very special level, and they began dating. The love angels helped him to reconnect with his own sensuality, which then worked its magic in leading him to find love with another person.

Practical Exercises with Archangel Raphael
(Channelling Emerald-green Light for Healing the Body)

Illness

To heal, you require healthy energy and love. My emerald-green light is available for your planet and contains the essence of healthy energy intertwined with love. To treat someone who is in pain, ask them to lie down as you stand or kneel behind them. Place your palms facing up and call me to your side with this invocation: 'Archangel Raphael, please come to my side and fill my body with your emerald-green light. Guide me to channel this into (name of person's) body so that they will be healed of their disease, disorder and discomfort. Thank you!'

Firstly, imagine your chakras blossoming as they are watered by the green light, and then place your hands just above the person's head and watch the energy flowing through, opening all chakras and healing the pain within their body. When this is finished, sweep through their aura and ask them to ground themselves by sitting upright and drinking water, as you also do the same.

Weight Problems

The amount of excess weight in your physical body is a reflection of the excess weight within your emotional body. Think about what your energies are hanging on to. Are you frightened to let go of them because you may not recognize yourself without them? Before any weight-loss programme can effectively work on your physical body, you must assess and change your energetic mental, emotional and spiritual bodies in order for any results that manifest themselves in the physical body can be sustained. Assess your thoughts, feelings and actions regarding the following memories you are carrying around with you: anxiety, neglect, guilt, exasperation and regret. These together develop into anger, which is one of the biggest causes of weight fluctuations. Those who are overweight are carrying excess unnecessary energy. Those who are underweight have no energy to carry on, as anger has turned into self-hatred. Release the anger within, and your weight will balance itself naturally. Ask for guidance and motivation to exercise frequently and cut away all attachments and patterns which need to be broken away from so that positive routines can form. It takes forty days to break habits and patterns, so ask for perseverance throughout this time.

Attractiveness

Each unique individual makes the world a beautiful place. Play your part is this beauty by adding your creative sparkle into your personality and how you present yourself. Conforming is conservative, being creative is constructive! When something is effortless, it is genuinely and naturally in its purest form. The most attractive quality that you can possess on all physical, mental, emotional and spiritual levels is purity. This quality brings out the best in others while also making the world a nicer place to live in and attracting more purity back into your life. If there is anything that you believe is not making you attractive, it is something that does not belong to your natural state. Channel the healing emerald-green light into this area and heal it with healthy energy and love. Have a clear-out of your wardrobe and design a completely new dress style, choosing certain colours which represent your character and personality. Practise the following exercise each time you walk into a group of people: fill your aura with golden Angel Starlight so you emanate love through your eyes, and smile. Notice how much attention and how many compliments you will receive!

Lethargy

For a very quick energy boost, rub your palms together for a few moments until they become warm, close your eyes and place your palms over each eye, allowing the heat and energy to go into your eyes. You may feel a tingly and warm sensation running into your eyes and down into your body. At the same time, take long deep breaths, in and out slowly, and ask that the Angels lift your energy levels throughout the day. Spend more time in nature, especially if you spend a lot of time working in a stressful city environment. Connect with trees, plants and, if possible, spend time in the sun to feel more energized and alive.

Sleep and Astral Travel

If you are finding it difficult to sleep, put some meditational music on, lie on your back and call the Angels of Sleep to send you off into a deep sleep by completely clearing your mind and sending warm, relaxing waves of energy through your body. Place a piece of rose quartz crystal or a gemstone under your pillow to help you connect with the angelic realm while you are asleep. Ask me, the Archangel of Travel, to watch over your journey from start to finish, removing all obstacles, delays and problems which may occur, so that your journey can be blessed, safe and stress-free. If you are lost, call for directions and guidance, and when other people magically appear, you will know that they have been directed by the angelic realm to assist you.

Depression

Depression is the feeling of sinking. Call upon me to channel the emerald-green light into your body and lift you back up again. Healing will be directed back into your past, going back from your present moment, year by year into your teenage years, your childhood and, if necessary, back into your previous lifetimes. Once you have consciously released all negative and hurtful memories, come back into your present moment now, with the memory of your past all healed, and begin a new chapter, starting from your present moment. Close your eyes and imagine happiness running through your entire body then extending out into your future, paving the way for a very bright life ahead. Hand over the situations which are causing depression in your life to the Angels by writing a brief explanation of the situation on paper, and place a photograph of the person who may be causing depression in your life with this paper in a green box or cloth for healing to take place. It is now out of your life and with the Angels.

Sensuality

Practise using your natural feminine or masculine qualities in your everyday life and you will learn to experience heightened pleasure in every moment. Take up dancing classes, or something similar, which allows you to express your sensuality and represents your identity in a beautiful and unique way. Enhance your connection with your partner by spending a few intimate moments gazing *through each other's eyes. Say the following daily prayer so that you can experience a sacred union with your twin soul: 'Dear Archangel Raphael, the Angel of Reunions, I ask that you guide me towards a very special and sacred reunion with my twin soul for my highest spiritual growth and evolution. Thank you!'*

PART VI:

ANGEL HEALING
FOR THE MIND

This section will cover the main mental challenges people face throughout their lives, especially with work and creativity. There will be a short description of the problems people encounter and how they are usually caused. The advice I give is directly channelled from the Angels, as they have a completely different perspective on the situations we find ourselves in. After each difficulty discussed, there is an Angel Healing meditation; practising these meditations will begin to release any blocks on an energetic level. The practical exercises provide ideas of any action to be taken and the affirmations for the mind will enhance your healing by changing your thought patterns into positivity.

The mind is made up of the subconscious mind and the conscious mind. Think of the subconscious as being like the software of a computer, running all your mental programmes – your memories, beliefs, fears, thought patterns and everything you perceive through your physical senses. The subconscious mind can also be regarded as your creative mind. It is the depository of your natural, inherent skills and talents, some of which you may not even be aware of yet.

On a physical level, it is responsible for automatic triggers such as breath control, reflexes and organ functions. On a spiritual level, it serves as your intuition and the way for you to access the unknown, such as the angelic realm or the spiritual realm. On an emotional level, it is responsible for triggering off your emotions to alert you about something and releasing certain chemicals into your body.

The subconscious mind cannot discern what is negative and what is positive. It just stores the piece of information until it can somehow serve a purpose in your life. Because these programmes are subliminal, i.e. hidden, they will have control over your behaviour and actions beyond your own conscious intentions. With Angel Healing techniques and meditations, you will be able to access your subconscious mind in order to acknowledge any negative programmes and make any necessary changes; this in turn will have a positive impact on your actions, and consequently on your life in general.

You can picture the conscious mind as being like the hard drive of a computer. Your awareness, logic and rationale come from this area of your mind. The conscious mind is not awake all the time, whereas the subconscious mind is. The conscious mind needs a chance to process all the new information it has absorbed throughout the day. Sleep is very important as it enables the mind to recuperate and function properly. Once the conscious mind has processed the information, most of it is transferred into and stored in the subconscious mind.

On a physical level, the conscious mind is responsible for providing instructions to your body so that you can undertake physical acts, for example, driving. On a spiritual level, it plays a role in processing instructions to help you open up to spirituality, aiding you in relaxation and in learning meditation techniques.

On an emotional level, it produces the sensations we are able to perceive and identify our emotions.

When altering your consciousness through Angel Healing, both left and right hemispheres of the brain synchronize. This enables the mind to relax and harmonize, which will improve your connection to and awareness of the Angels. It also helps with concentration, focus, using your imagination and sensing the Angel Starlight.

Work is an exchange of giving and receiving. For many people, work has become monotonous and they resent giving too much of themselves, their time, their lives, just in order to survive. The Angels want to help to bring back that balance to Earth by evening out the financial abundance throughout the world as people tap into their creative abilities to create the work that makes them happy.

Angel Healing allows and helps each person to find their hidden, dormant, creative abilities and use them as 'work'. The biggest and most important factor to remember is, when you do your work with passion, you naturally radiate love and joy which will attract clients, customers and employees to your work, effortlessly. Provide a service that is necessary to others, through love. At this moment in life, what people need most are hope, direction, love and security. If you can use your creative imagination, you can make a difference to the world on a large scale, plus doing what you love, you are immediately successful. Provide a happy, joyful, purposeful workplace for people to put their passion into and earn you more business and abundance. Imagine a company with energetic and enthusiastic employees who do not compete against or put each other down, in fact they inspire each other to succeed! You do not need to spend or charge millions in order to be successful – you need to reach out and touch millions of lives and hearts! If you currently work in a company and feel unappreciated, review the company's mission. What are their goals, where do they use their creativity? Change the way you think through Angel Healing and tap into your amazing creative mind to remove the unnecessary fears and blocks that hold you back. Make the universe your employer, the Angels your colleagues and the world your customers. If everyone was to use their creativity and had the intention of bringing love into lives, the world would balance out evenly and the feeling of working to survive would end. Take your power back and love what you do for a living.

Positive Thinking

Programmes

Mental programmes are held within your mind's software, the subconscious mind. The subconscious mind cannot ascertain whether any particular programme is positive or negative. These programmes trigger emotions, so if they are negative, they will make you feel negative about yourself or your situation. Mental programmes also determine your actions and behaviour. Programmes are deeply hidden, therefore they cannot be accessed through logic. When you behave in certain ways which you know are not serving you in the best way and are causing you unhappiness, there is a negative programme working its influence. Angels will help you to access and change these negative programmes when you alter your conscious awareness through deep relaxation during meditation. These programmes must be changed on an energetic level rather than simply covering up the negative. An example of one negative programme may be formulated in the phrase: 'Happiness is difficult to achieve.' Angels will change this thought pattern into the most suitable positive programme, i.e., 'Happiness is everyone's right.' You will then start believing that you deserve and are worthy of happiness like everyone else is. Once you believe this, your thoughts regarding happiness will be a lot more positive, and your actions and emotions will reflect this belief.

Beliefs

Programmes generate beliefs and beliefs generate thoughts. Your belief system is formed by everything you learn from life experiences, previous lifetimes and group consciousness and everything that your conscious mind perceives to be real. Your beliefs are statements which begin 'I am', 'I do', 'I have', 'I know', etc. Depending on how limiting, negative and fearful your belief systems are, you will act accordingly, therefore you will have emotions and situations reflecting these beliefs. An example of a limited belief is 'I will never be happy.' Angels want you to know that it is your divine right to be happy in this present moment, not once you have achieves all your goals some time in the future. During Angel Healing, the Angels will transmute your negative belief into 'I am happy now and always.' Transforming your belief system will have an enormous impact on your inner peace, happiness and success.

Thoughts

Negative thoughts about yourself, your life or others hold very low energetic frequencies, which either stay within your angelic body or are directed into your life, or to people or situations. When they are held within yourself, they tend to accumulate and become a natural way of thinking for you. Unfortunately, negative thinking is a way of sabotaging any potential of achieving success in any area of your life and also has an impact on your physical, emotional and spiritual well-being. Angels will help you to become aware of your negative thought patterns and will guide you to consciously take control of your mind. Positive thinking may seem out of the ordinary or even false when you first start changing your mindset. This is because there will be a conflict between what your subconscious mind believes and what the conscious mind is trying to believe. A positive thought such as 'Today everybody will be happy' will influence your angelic body's energetic frequency and therefore will be sending out the signals or vibes into your external world, therefore creating a very happy environment.

ANGEL HEALING MEDITATION FOR POSITIVE THINKING

ANGEL SECRET:

'Amend the way you think so that the things you think about will mend.'

CROWN CHAKRA

Angel Starlight enters your angelic body through a beautiful white rose just above your physical body. You see a silvery sparkling star in the centre of your crown chakra and connect with your soul. Your Guardian Angel now guides you to become fully aware of your thoughts. Take a moment to observe your thought patterns and listen to your internal self talk. Do not try to control what is happening; just allow them to be. Each thought leaves your mind and gets sent into the air as bubbles.

THIRD-EYE CHAKRA

Angel Starlight travels down into the purple rose between your two eyes and into your mind. It now begins to clear your intuition blocks. Your Guardian Angel now shows you a cloud forming, made up of all the thoughts that are being processed from your mind. The more you think, the larger this cloud grows. Notice how bright or dull this cloud is, depending on how positive or negative your thoughts are. Gradually you see that this cloud is being split into two parts: a dark cloud for all negative thoughts and a bright cloud of positive thoughts. Notice the difference in size and density of the two clouds now hovering above you.

THROAT CHAKRA

Angel Starlight travels down into the blue rose in your throat and extends towards your ears. Your Guardian Angel now asks you to talk about how you feel about what you see, either in your mind or out loud. How does the dark cloud make you feel? Are you surprised at how many negative thoughts you have? Are they really necessary? What area of your life are you having the most negative thoughts about? What or who are your negative influences?

HEART CHAKRA

Angel Starlight travels down into the green rose within your heart and, as it blossoms, you see that it slowly transforms into a pink rose. Your Guardian Angel now asks you to feel the responsibility for the dark cloud of negativity that you have created and take control of what happens to it. Now that it has taken some form of existence, it has to be directed somewhere or transmuted into light. You now feel unconditional love coming from your heart and being directed into the dark cloud until it completely dissipates.

SOLAR PLEXUS CHAKRA

Angel Starlight travels down into the yellow rose within your stomach area, the core of your being. Your Guardian Angel shows you a list of programmes regarding the area of your life where you are experiencing challenges at the moment. As you become aware of each negative programme, see that it gets rewritten and re-stored in your mind with positive wording, beginning with changing the patterns underlying the formulation 'Negative thinking is part of my life' to 'Positive thinking is beneficial for my well-being.'

SACRAL CHAKRA

Angel Starlight travels down into the orange rose just below your navel and activates your creative abilities. Your Guardian Angel brings your awareness back to the bright cloud of positive thoughts. Using your creative energy, direct this cloud into the universe and see that it acts like a magnet, attaching itself to a positive situation, person, place or object and bringing it back into your presence.

ROOT CHAKRA

Angel Starlight travels down into the red rose at the base of your spine. Visualize that you are now at your most positive state and believe that you have manifested into your reality exactly what you positively believe that you deserve. See that you are living, breathing, feeling and immersing yourself in your desires. Your subconscious mind believes that your visualization is your actual reality, and the more positive thoughts you have surrounding this situation, the more positive emotions you have and the higher you are raising your energetic frequencies in order to physically attract it into your life. Repeat the affirmation: 'I choose only to have positive thoughts.'

Success Story

Helena had Angel Healing to change her mind frame and thinking patterns. She had grown up in a family which, unfortunately, had a tendency always to think the worst. She found it extremely difficult to relax and to focus her mind in her meditation. The

Angels explained that she was over-analytical and therefore unable to gain clarity and concentration. Helena felt extremely frustrated, as each time she tried to meditate, her mind would wander off in different directions, and then she would fall asleep. However, as she was very sensitive to the energy about her, she had no problem feeling when her Guardian Angel was there and trying to help her. She was given a mind-clearing exercise to carry out each night. She was either to hold a clear quartz crystal in her hand or to place it under her pillow while closing her eyes and visualizing her thoughts as cars driving through her mind. She would see many thoughts passing through very quickly, and she was to slow them down with her intention and focus. As they slowed down, the thoughts would become fewer and fewer until she would only see one thought that she wanted to hang on to, and that could be any positive thought or statement that she would look at in her mind and repeat over and over again. This technique was given to her by her Guardian Angel in order to help her enhance her relaxation and meditation skills. Helena found this very helpful and practised it every night. This has completely changed her way of thinking and as a result she is attracting more positive situations and outcomes than she has ever done before.

Overcoming Fears

What is Fear?

Fear limits your body, mind, heart and soul from fully expressing love. The suppression of love turns into anger and frustration that you are not achieving happiness. The Angels can see the fears you have through your eyes, which truly are the windows to your soul. They urge you to confront and release your fears so that you can feel freedom. The emotion you need in order to do achieve this goal is trust. Whether your fear is deeply embedded in your subconscious mind or you are fully and consciously aware, it will continue to appear in your life as a block until it is healed. Angel Healing empowers you to take control of your fears by assuring you that you have the full support and encouragement of your Guardian Angel and at the same time will be protected when you ask for their intervention to remove your fears. When working on healing fear, Angels will guide you in the best way to actually understand where, when, why and how your fear was created in the first place. Only when you fully understand the origin of your fear, can you fully let go.

Influence

Angels know that our lives are heavily influenced and even driven by fear. The energy of fear creates a lack of control within you which then filters into your life. There is so much competition in the world for control, which is obtained by disempowering others with fear of the consequences if they do not follow. By taking your power back, by asserting that you are ready to take control of your life, you send out the energy and vibes from within to your external world. Angels want you to follow the profound wisdom you have within yourself and not be influenced in a negative way by your external world. This way you are positively influencing your external world and being empowered to create the life you want without the limitations imposed by fear.

Hidden Fears

Some fears are deeply hidden within your subconscious mind and only present themselves when triggered by certain emotions. This type of fear is created by a traumatic event, or events, which occurred at some point and has left a memory within your emotional body. An example of a hidden fear could be the fear of being judged by others. This could have been created when you were a child, as a response to the feeling of having been humiliated by others. This may have left an emotional scar and had a negative impact on your confidence and the way you are perceived by others. Although you may have forgotten about the incident itself, the memory still resides deep within you. On a conscious level, you may now think you don't care what people think of you. However, the deep-rooted fear of being judged will hold you back, without your even being aware that this is the cause, from taking the appropriate actions that could improve your life, or stop your personal self-development.

Healing Fears

With Angel Healing, you can easily find, confront and release the fears that hold you back from happiness. If you are aware of your fear and feel ready to let it go, your Angels will take you on an inward journey to identify what aspect of love is missing within you. Fear is an illusion created through lack of love. Angels will guide you to fill the voids within you and make you feel whole, complete and empowered to confront and let go of your fear. For example, if you have a fear of flying, you may be lacking the energy of control. Look at the areas of your life in which you lack control in. In order to deal with your fear of flying, for example, Angels will help you to get back in touch with your inner power and will transmute the negative energy caused by fear into control, as well as trust, peace and whatever else may be lacking.

ANGEL HEALING MEDITATION FOR OVERCOMING FEARS

ANGEL SECRET:

'The darkness of fear disappears when the light of love appears.'

CROWN CHAKRA

Angel Starlight enters your angelic body through a beautiful white rose just above your physical body. You see a silvery sparkling star in the centre of your crown chakra and connect with your soul. Your Guardian Angel now wraps its wings around your body, comforting and supporting you as you prepare to heal your fear.

THIRD-EYE CHAKRA

Angel Starlight travels down into the purple rose between your two eyes and into your mind. It now begins to clear your intuition blocks. Your Guardian Angel asks you to think about your fear and how it is holding you back in life. Keep asking yourself 'If I confront my fear, what will happen? What is the worst-case scenario?', until you get to that very last scenario. You may realize that none of these scenarios will ever actually happen, it is just that your mind has been conditioned to believe that they will. Visualize the golden Angel Starlight running through all these negative beliefs until it gets all the way to the negative pro-gramme creating them.

THROAT CHAKRA

Angel Starlight travels down into the blue rose in your throat and extends towards your ears. Your Guardian Angel now asks you to think back into your past until you find the situation that caused your fear. It may have been a situation you experienced in your own life, witnessed in another person's life, or another external factor. If you intuitively feel as if this fear may originate in something in a past life, see yourself being taken back in time before this incarnation. Once you locate this memory, see that all negative aspects of the situation are transmuted and healed.

HEART CHAKRA

Angel Starlight travels down into the green rose within your heart and, as it blossoms, you see that it slowly transforms into a pink rose. Your Guardian Angel now asks you to feel the effects that this fear is having on your heart and body. As you feel the effects of your fear building up within your heart and body, the Angel Starlight runs through you, calming your nerves and releasing your tension.

SOLAR PLEXUS CHAKRA

Angel Starlight travels down into the yellow rose within your stomach area, the core of your being. Your Guardian Angel now brings your awareness to your inner power, which is a shining golden sphere in the centre of your solar plexus chakra. Visualize and feel this solid ball of power expanding within you, giving you the confidence and strength you require to confront and release your fear. Now take yourself back to the root cause of your fear and listen to yourself as an empowered person taking control of the situation physically, mentally and emotionally, and spiritually standing firm against it.

SACRAL CHAKRA

Angel Starlight travels down into the orange rose just below your navel and activates your creative abilities. Your Guardian Angel now guides you to use your creative energy to visualize yourself living your life without this fear holding you back and that everything will work out perfectly. Ask your Guardian Angel for guidance and assistance to deal with any obstacles or doubts that may appear in your mind, or when you feel the fear creeping back in.

ROOT CHAKRA

Angel Starlight travels down into the red rose at the base of your spine. Bring your awareness to your mind and repeat the affirmation: 'I am now moving forward without fear holding me back.' Visualize yourself in the near future, living your life without the restrictions that your old fear used to inflict in your life.

Success Story

Jackie had Angel Healing in order to overcome her fear of flying. During her meditation, the Angels asked her questions in order to delve into where this fear originated. Jackie hadn't always had this fear, as she had travelled by plane throughout her teenage years, frequently going abroad on holiday. Her fear had begun after a very traumatic experience in her life which left her feeling powerless and insecure. Since then, she had become quite obsessive and controlling. The Angels explained that, every time a situation arose in which she was unable to be completely in control, negative memories were evoked in her mind, and these affected her emotions and physical well-being. She agreed with this, and recalled that she had suffered from mild panic attacks and would lash out at people in order to protect herself. The healing energy started to run through her body, mind, heart and soul, transforming all negative associations to do with power and control. This allowed her to take a step back and to believe and trust that she was protected. Although Jackie needed a few sessions before she was able to face flying again, her obsessive, controlling and aggressive behaviour changed almost immediately.

Having a Successful Career

Unhappiness

You may have negative thoughts about your current career. This may be because you are not fully expressing your skills and talents. When you are not expressing what you are best at, you feel mentally suppressed, which leads to feeling physically trapped, therefore you will find it difficult to enjoy your work, let alone succeed in it. When you do the work you love most, you will naturally love your work! Passion comes from love, and success comes from passion. Angels can help you to create harmony in your current career, even if you are unhappy. This will give you the energy you need to keep going until you are ready to move forward into a career that you are more suited to. You are more likely to be happy and successful in a field that you understand and believe in, rather than one that makes you feel unappreciated or worthless. Your inner thoughts and emotions shine through to your life, and others, including colleagues and managers, perceive this negative energy and will therefore react towards you accordingly. When you are passionate about working, this will show in your application, interview and appraisals. The real secret to happiness and fulfilment is being passionate, or at least being at peace, in every moment. There is no rule that says you cannot explore your preferred career while you are in your current career. You may have to balance your time and energy efficiently, especially if you have other commitments, however is well worth the investment. As you are building up your knowledge, experience and reputation, you are laying down the foundations to make the transition. You are not much use to your current employer if you are unhappy, and you are not achieving personal success either.

Transition

You will be guided to take the leap of faith when the time is right. There is not much point leaving one company and going into another one if it remains in the field of work that you no longer want to do. There is a misconception that people sometimes drive you out of a job, rather than the actual work itself. If you change the way you think, and understand that people are actually reacting to the vibes you are sending from the inside out, this concept is incorrect. If you move to a new workplace to do the same job, and it doesn't fit with your creative abilities, you will not send out happy vibes and eventually your new colleagues will react to you in the same way your old colleagues did. This sort of transition is escapism and will only delay the actual career transition you need.

Through Angel Healing, you will locate the fears and limiting beliefs which are stopping you from making the transition into your chosen field. More than likely, it will be fear of not being financially secure, or fear of change. Angel Healing gives you the opportunity to look at and resolve these negative mindsets in the most positive way. Once these are healed and transmuted into positivity, your energy frequency will rise and project different vibes into your current workplace. Instead of feeling suppressed or trapped, you will start feeling more in control of your life, and hopeful, as you will start to believe that it is you who makes the choices which determine your success rather than depending on others to dictate how well you are doing. When you explore the possibilities of working for yourself rather than working for others, your natural instinct is to give it your full attention and lots of positive energy, and to channel your passion into making it a success. When you are in a more positive frame of mind, you can think about how you can make a sensible transition between careers, into one that will allow you to express your creative skills and where you could excel by giving your work your full commitment.

Security

Angels understand the need for financial security, so they will never guide you to take drastic or unrealistic actions before thinking things through. Your transition from unhappiness to happiness in your career can start immediately, as soon as you change the way you look at things. While you are in a career that is not stimulating you in the best way, look for opportunities to work on your weaknesses. Ask your Guardian Angel every day to give you patience as you go through your transition and to guide you each step of the way. Your Angels will not allow you to make this decision until it is your divine timing, i.e. it is in line with your life plan. Many people have fears about security and have a belief that creative or independent work may not be as secure and successful as working for a big or established organization nine to five. This belief may seem logical, however it is usually based on fear, and in many cases it involves a sacrifice of your happiness, your sense of freedom and your own personal achievement.

Challenges

Any challenges you may be faced with in your present career are vehicles for your personal growth and development; attaining this level of growth and development are necessary for you to make you a success in your preferred career. Challenges may occur because you are in an environment that does not match your own energetic frequency. For example, your calling may be to help or teach people, however your current role may completely contradict your values. This will create a clash within you internally, which will manifest itself externally, mainly through conflict with your colleagues or clients. The best way to handle this situation is to change your focus from being a victim to being a student; learning about people and how to interact with them. If you seem to clash with people in the workplace even if you have moved companies a few times, more than likely there are mental programmes founded in memories from how you were treated before and a fear of it happening again.

Values

Each person has a unique set of values, and they prioritize them as an individual, depending on their beliefs and life experience. Values will motivate and influence you to act according to them, as they are the standards of how you choose to live life. Relationships with others are determined on your values, and although another individual will never have exactly the same set of values and place them in the same order of importance, for relationships to have some substance, mutual respect for others' values is needed. In the workplace, there can be a huge divide in value systems between colleagues. Some would put financial reward as a top priority, whereas others would prioritize personal achievement; impressing others; using their skills; interacting with people; or see work as a break from the pressures of family life. Clashes in values are a huge factor in unhappiness at work. Ask your Angel to help you create a list of your different values in life, relationships and work. Be honest. When you have completed this list, review how you live your life, the dynamics of your relationships and your career. Do they fit in line with your list, or are you not being true to your values? This is the way to measure your true happiness and, in terms of work, to find out to which career or area of work you would be most suited.

Change

In order to change your outer world, you must first change your inner world. If you want to make a change in your life, you need to make a change in yourself. Change may seem scary if you have been in the same situation for a very long time. Sometimes it's easier to plod along or stay in a comfort zone than make a huge change to better your life. If you are prepared to go on a journey from your current state to your preferred state, you must firstly have a very clear picture of your goal and the desired outcome before your Angels can guide you along that path. Whatever you focus on is what you achieve, therefore if you do not have clarity, your focus will be blurred and the outcome is confusion, which then manifests into the emotion of frustration. A build-up of frustration creates stress. If you ask them for guidance, Angels will show you the best direction to take at the best time. Any blocks or obstacles can only be overcome when you begin to take action.

ANGEL HEALING MEDITATION FOR HAVING A SUCCESSFUL CAREER

ANGEL SECRET:

'Work on love and you'll love to work.'

CROWN CHAKRA

Angel Starlight enters your angelic body through a beautiful white rose just above your physical body. You see a silvery sparkling star in the centre of your crown chakra and connect with your soul. Your Guardian Angel now asks you to think about your current career. Observe your negative thoughts, beliefs and programmes regarding work, and visualize them forming into a dark cloud above your body. Your Guardian Angel now transmutes this negative dark cloud with the Angel Starlight energy until it completely dissipates.

THIRD-EYE CHAKRA

Angel Starlight travels down into the purple rose between your two eyes and into your mind. It now begins to clear your intuition blocks. Your Guardian Angel shows you a vision of yourself in the workplace from a third person's point of view. Look at your presentation, behaviour, body language, communication and your aura. With this opportunity to view yourself, how do you think you can improve? Using your intuition, can you see why colleagues react to you in certain ways and what their perception of you is? Are you approachable, or do you have barriers up which stop effective communication?

THROAT CHAKRA

Angel Starlight travels down into the blue rose in your throat and extends towards your ears. Communicate your observation to your Guardian Angel now and ask for assistance in improving what you don't like in your own actions. By assessing your weaknesses, you are able to break bad habits and patterns which add to or cause unhappiness in your current work environment.

HEART CHAKRA

Angel Starlight travels down into the green rose within your heart and, as it blossoms, you see that it slowly transforms into a pink rose. Your Guardian Angel now guides you to be completely true to yourself about your career. As you go deeper into your heart, feel how unhappy you are on a scale of 1 to 10, 10 being the unhappiest. What would counteract this unhappiness? What is missing? Feel this positive energy filling your heart now and expanding throughout your angelic body.

SOLAR PLEXUS CHAKRA

Angel Starlight travels down into the yellow rose within your stomach area, the core of your being. Your Guardian Angel directs the Angel Starlight into your current workplace, transmuting the negative energy in the building and also clearing the negative cords between you and colleagues. Connect with your inner power to help you through career transitions, if this is the correct path for you to take. If it isn't the time for you to move on, your Guardian Angel will give you the energies of patience and tolerance as you utilize your time in your current workplace effectively. This means working on your weaknesses and learning from each situation you are faced with.

SACRAL CHAKRA

Angel Starlight travels down into the orange rose just below your navel and activates your creative abilities. Your Guardian Angel now shows you how you can create happiness in your working life rather than being unhappy. As you connect with your creative energy, you will be shown your natural skills and talents which should be used in conjunction with your career. They may be hidden somewhere deep within you and may have not been explored until now. See them resurfacing and ask for guidance on how you could best develop your abilities and knowledge.

ROOT CHAKRA

Angel Starlight travels down into the red rose at the base of your spine. Visualize that you are working within the career of your dreams, where you are completely free to control your success, and that you are very well respected in your field. As you excel within your position, you become an idol for many people, who look up to you and see you as an inspiration. By feeling gratitude for the journey you have been on until this moment, you are rewarded with an abundance of success, wealth and happiness.

Success Story

After completing my education, I was unsure which career to follow. I didn't have a passion for anything at the time, and didn't feel drawn to further education in any particular field. With the guidance of my family, I went into the financial sector, as this seemed to provide security and was a respectable place to work. I began at a financial-company call centre, progressed into retail banking in a branch and then progressed further, into corporate and investment banking in the City. Each new job opportunity played a huge part in my personal development and, along the way, I made friends and met people who have completely changed my life and inspired me in amazing ways. However, I never felt settled for long; I usually became aware of a feeling of wanting to move on after two or so years of being in a company. As I developed my personality and found my true identity, I realized that the field I was working in no longer complemented me and was not in line with my truth. While continuing with my day job, which involved long, stressful days, I studied in the evenings and at weekends to qualify as a practitioner in different healing therapies. After three years, my courses of study were complete and I began teaching and working part time, as well as keeping my full-time job. Surprisingly, doing my healing work every evening after a stressful day in the bank energized me. In order to smooth the transition between my careers and not risk my financial security in the process, I worked hard for years to build up my client base and reputation. Only after this did I feel that the time was right for me to leave the financial sector and do the healing work I loved full time. Throughout this journey, I have had angelic guidance, assistance and healing, and I believe that, without this, the transformation of my career and my life would have been impossible.

Creativity

Co-Creator

You carry the powerful energy of creation within you. Therefore you are a co-creator and there is nothing you cannot create in your life. When you decide to make a change in your life, you are able to tap into this creative energy and use it wisely, with the guidance of your intuition and of the Angels to create the change you desire. Angel Healing gives you the opportunity to remove the negativity within and around you so that you can believe in your own power as well as your creative abilities. No matter what your role in life is, you are equally as important as anyone else and can make a change on any scale that you wish, whether it is changing your own life for the better or influencing millions of others with your creativity, skills and talents. Those who are in the limelight are aware of their abilities and are using them for their own benefit. In turn, they are providing entertainment, knowledge, beauty and many more positive influencing factors into millions of lives.

Creative Expression

Angels can help you to find creative energy and abilities and ways to express them through your skills and talents. They will guide you towards new opportunities, or they will guide opportunities to you. As new doors open to enable you to do what you are best at, your confidence will improve, which will lead to happiness. By sharing your unique creativity, you play a role in creating a happier and more joyful world. Joy is a very healing energy and, experiencing it and living your life in joy, you will indirectly be contributing to healing others' lives. Creativity can be expressed in many different forms, for example in colourful, beautiful and attractive clothes, or in the design of your home or objects within it and around you. As your outer world reflects into your inner world, these things make a huge difference on your personal feelings. Music, singing and dance are also forms of creative expression which positively influences others' feelings.

Creative Visualization

The list of what we can create with our imagination is endless, and this is why creative visualization through meditation exercises is very beneficial. Creative visualization means impressing your desires on your subconscious mind and watching yourself actually already having, being and living it. This magically changes the energetic frequencies within your angelic body and starts sending positive vibes into your outer world. When opportunities are presented to you by the universe, you will take full advantage of them. Your subconscious mind is not aware of what your reality is or is not, so the more you visualize something taking place, the more you reprogramme outdated negative beliefs. Although affirmations are very useful at programming your mind, visualizing and feeling as if you have already created your desires is even more powerful. How long it takes to actually see your results in physical form depends on your emotions, which are the driving force of your creativity. The amount of trust, positivity and faith you have in this process will influence the speed of the outcome, and the help of your Guardian Angel along the way will remove all doubts, hidden obstacles and blocks on your energy.

Creative Blocks

Each person has at least one very unique quality that needs to be expressed. Suppressing your creative energy will lead to frustration and a sense of being unfulfilled or an under-achiever. You may have been aware of your creative talents as a child but perhaps you did not receive the recognition, reassurance or encouragement to develop them. When this energy is lying dormant within you for a long time, the fear of expression and failure will manifest itself in a creative block. The fear of humiliation or judgement will hold you back and have a negative impact on your confidence, blocking you from even trying. Angels will help you to confront and release the negative programmes or fears that are causing the creative block. They will also help you to get back in touch with your natural confidence to express your creativity. The Angel Starlight will run through your angelic body and chakras to remove stagnant energy on all levels, especially within the sacral chakra. Ask your Guardian Angel to give you motivation and energy so that you can get organized and allow your creativity to flow once they have healed your fears.

Creative Channelling

If any of your chakras become blocked with negative energy, your natural creativity becomes suppressed. Angels will help you with the creativity channelling process by relaxing you by means of Angel Healing exercises like meditation. This will allow you to connect to your intuition for guidance, and to use your imagination. Creativity starts with an imagination in your subconscious mind, which is then processed by your conscious mind. Angels will see the process through until it manifests into your reality, and will bring your attention to where the blocks are held. Blocks such as feeling that you have no time are programmes in your mind which can be changed so that you find ways of making time available, by re-evaluating your list of prioritized values. A very effective way of channelling your creativity is through writing. When you relax your conscious mind and allow your Guardian Angel to write through you, you will be amazed at the information that comes through. It's the same with singing: when you allow the energy of a group of Angels to sing through your throat chakra, you and those listening to you will experience something Heavenly.

ANGEL HEALING MEDITATION FOR CREATIVITY

ANGEL SECRET:

'Imagination holds the image of your desire; creativity shows the activity you require.'

CROWN CHAKRA

Angel Starlight enters your angelic body through a beautiful white rose just above your physical body. You see a silvery sparkling star in the centre of your crown chakra and connect with your soul. Visualize yourself reaching out to make a connection with the universal energy of creation. A beam of brilliant white light shines in through your crown chakra, connecting with your soul.

THIRD-EYE CHAKRA

Angel Starlight travels down into the purple rose between your two eyes and into your mind. It now begins to clear your intuition blocks. Visualize and feel that a beautiful eye is opening deep within your third-eye chakra. Through this eye, you see the bright light of the universal energy of creation building a scene in your mind of what you wish to create in your life. Hold the images very clearly in your mind's eye and focus on the specific details of the scene.

THROAT CHAKRA

Angel Starlight travels down into the blue rose in your throat and extends towards your ears. Your Guardian Angel now guides you to communicate your imagination, beginning by saying, 'I want this in my life now,' and to speak about what it is that you are creating in detail. Once you have finished speaking about your creation, you will begin to channel information from your Guardian Angel, which will give you specific information about when this will come into your life physically and some advice about what action you need to take.

HEART CHAKRA

Angel Starlight travels down into the green rose within your heart and, as it blossoms, you see that it slowly transforms into a pink rose. Your Guardian Angel asks you to bring the vision created by the universal energy of creation down into your heart. Energize this vision with all the passion you hold within your heart. Feel that you are adding substance and love into your creation.

SOLAR PLEXUS CHAKRA

Angel Starlight travels down into the yellow rose within your stomach area, the core of your being. Your Guardian Angel now asks you to bring the vision created by the universal energy of creation through your heart and down into your stomach. The Angel Starlight energy is now transmuting any apprehension into complete confidence and the belief that you have the ability to create this situation into your physical reality.

SACRAL CHAKRA

Angel Starlight travels down into the orange rose just below your navel and activates your creative abilities. Your Guardian Angel asks you to bring the vision created by the universal energy of creation through your stomach and down into your sacral area of expression. Visualize yourself expressing the joy, happiness and success that your creation will bring into your life. Your Guardian Angel now shows you how you can use your creative abilities to spread the energy of joy, happiness and success into your world. As you relax deeply, affirm: 'I am a powerful creator' and watch this belief reprogramming all existing negative or limiting beliefs regarding your creative abilities.

ROOT CHAKRA

Angel Starlight travels down into the red rose at the base of your spine. Your Guardian Angel shows you that you are living your dream scenario every day of your life and that you are an inspirational creative director within your field of work. You are in control of creating your life. This includes the way you allow the past to create your present moment and the way you allow your present moment to create the future. You are a powerful creator.

Success Story

Tess came to me for an Angel Reading and Healing session because she was feeling trapped and blocked in her career. During her meditation, I guided her to the past in order to find where and when the block had originated. In the meditation, the Angels showed me that she was very suppressed and felt unable to express her true identity and creativity, and also that she needed to forgive people from the past in order to move into her desired future. She told me that, as a child, she had loved singing but was not encouraged by her family to pursue this. In fact, a few times, she had been laughed at, which really hurt her feelings and knocked her confidence. The Angels wanted to heal this negative memory and encourage her to follow her dreams – especially as it became clear that singing was related to her life purpose: she would bring healing to others through her voice. After her Angel Healing session, she knew that the feelings and passion she once had for music and singing was the right path for her to follow. It set things in motion, and she began recording songs, found the right producer for her and is well on her way to achieving her goals.

Confidence

Self-Discovery

To be truly confident, you must be true to yourself. This means knowing yourself fully, by assessing your strengths and your weaknesses. It also means becoming aware of your unique beauty and the value that you bring to life. The Angels will take you on a self-discovery journey when you ask for their guidance. You will come to know your true self by understanding the language of your subconscious mind, your behaviour, your beliefs and emotions – everything that is going on within your inner world. This leads to self-mastery and confidence in each step you take. Knowing your true self means finding and living as your authentic, uninfluenced, pure and unique self. The journey of self-discovery may last a whole lifetime, however self-acceptance can start immediately. Effective relationships with other people will teach you a lot about yourself, as they bring up factors that may not be within your own awareness. Although it may seem as if you are being judged, or even insulted by others, listening to constructive criticism without becoming defensive is beneficial on your self-discovery journey. Asking your Angels to remove any negative emotions or influences caused by others will help you to identify and live as your true self.

Self-Belief

Once you begin your journey of self-discovery, you may come to realize your insecurities and, by digging a bit deeper, you can get to the causes of these insecurities, which may have been held in your mind for a very long time. When you are being true to yourself, Angels will help you to confront the things that you are not happy about. They will help and guide you not to be so harsh on yourself and, instead, to believe in your purity. This means holding the purest intentions, thoughts, emotions and plans towards yourself and others at all times. No matter what seems to be wrong in your life, or in the way in which others are treating you, it's about always remaining true to yourself. When you come from this place, you take full responsibility for your inner world and it is from this that self-belief arises. True self-belief means that you are not covering up your faults or insecurities and just pretending to be confident. What you are doing is acknowledging that something negative has somehow managed to override your natural positive state of being. Living without self-belief creates within you a negative outlook on yourself and therefore sends negative energetic frequencies into your life, which leads to negative reactions from others. Angel Healing begins from the inner world and reflects into the outside world.

Self-Respect

Once you believe in yourself, you will be able to respect yourself for all that you are. You will be able to appreciate your strengths and accept your weaknesses without being caught up in others' judgement or opinion of you. Self-respect comes by holding on to your own integrity no matter what experiences you are faced with in life. Your power comes from self-respect. Being comfortable with others' judgements of you will give you a feeling of freedom. Angels see that we place far too much energy into conforming to the rules of society in order to fit in and not be judged in a negative way. The fear of being judged stems from a deeper fear of not being loved, then from a fear of being lonely, and so on. Being judged in a negative way makes people feel isolated and as if they are not accepted by others. Angels will help you to be strong enough emotionally and to stand your ground with self-respect while showing respect to others.

Self-Confidence

Angels say that self-confidence means knowing your worth, believing in your values and respecting yourself fully. The secret of confidence is finding the balance between all of the above without arrogance. When you react to situations with a pure heart in every situation, nothing can harm your confidence. Confidence does not need to be projected in a certain way for it to be real. Quiet confidence is powerful and genuine, as you are not seeking external approval for your behaviour or the way you are. Overconfidence is sometimes an act formulated because a person is seeking approval, love or to conceal their insecurities. Angels will help you to find the perfect balance of confidence and to project it from the inside out. They will guide you to set the foundations for lasting confidence, which are self-discovery, self-belief and self-respect. Insecurities arise from feelings of inadequacy when you compare yourself to others, and, unfortunately, they build up over time and completely diminish your personal confidence. Angels know your inner, deepest feelings and never judge you for having them. They gently guide you to acknowledge and confront your insecurities while boosting your morale with healing energy. Confidence comes from believing that you are able to deal with any situation, and learning and growing from your mistakes. Unshakable confidence is absolute inner peace.

ANGEL HEALING MEDITATION FOR CONFIDENCE

ANGEL SECRET:

'Confidence is believing and trusting in your purity.'

CROWN CHAKRA

Angel Starlight enters your angelic body through a beautiful white rose just above your physical body. You see a silvery sparkling star in the centre of your crown chakra and connect with your soul. Your Guardian Angel now holds a huge mirror up in front of you. As you take a good look at yourself on the exterior, you will begin to see aspects you are not so happy about. Each time you hear yourself saying inside: 'I don't like this because', ask your Guardian Angel to help you look deeper into that aspect. Think about why you do not like that particular aspect of yourself and learn to accept it. Visualize the golden Angel Starlight energy going into that area of your body, transmuting the build-up of negative thoughts into positive ones.

THIRD-EYE CHAKRA

Angel Starlight travels down into the purple rose between your two eyes and into your mind. It now begins to clear your intuition blocks. Your Guardian Angel asks you to see yourself in the perfect image of what you want to be, with no faults – perfection in every way. See yourself through the eyes of an Angel, and look deeper into your heart and soul to connect with your magnificence and uniqueness. From this moment onwards, you will only recognize your true self and your inner beauty will be allowed to shine through as confidence.

THROAT CHAKRA

Angel Starlight travels down into the blue rose in your throat and extends towards your ears. Your Guardian Angel now asks that all the negative beliefs you have that are stopping you from being completely confident will be expressed and reprogrammed into positive statements. Repeat these affirmations of your new positive beliefs and visualize a major programme represented by the phrase 'Confidence comes naturally' being embedded deep into your subconscious mind.

HEART CHAKRA

Angel Starlight travels down into the green rose within your heart and, as it blossoms, you see that it slowly transforms into a pink rose. Your Guardian Angel opens your heart and transmutes the heartbreak you have experienced over many years due to low confidence in all areas of your life. Visualize your heart becoming whole again with complete and utter love towards yourself and others.

SOLAR PLEXUS CHAKRA

Angel Starlight travels down into the yellow rose within your stomach area, the core of your being. Your Guardian Angel directs the Angel Starlight into your stomach area until you feel extremely empowered. This is the area of your power, and real confidence creates power. Visualize a golden sphere shining brightly every time you need to tap into your confidence.

SACRAL CHAKRA

Angel Starlight travels down into the orange rose just below your navel and activates your creative abilities. Your Guardian Angel creates a confidence meter which runs from your heart down into your sacral chakra. Using your creative imagination, you are able to visualize the amount of confidence you are exuding. The perfect balance is at your centre, where your solar plexus chakra is. When your confidence level is higher and closer to your heart chakra, you are being too compassionate. However, when your confidence levels are below your solar plexus chakra, you may be reacting with arrogance. Always monitor your confidence levels when faced with any situation, and keep your self-respect.

ROOT CHAKRA

Angel Starlight travels down into the red rose at the base of your spine. Your Guardian Angel now takes you on a journey back into your past and you remember all situations which led you to feel overpowered by others' confidence. As you relive these times, your Guardian Angel transmutes into positive the negative memories and energies within you which have created limited beliefs about your confidence and worthiness. See that you behave in a more confident way, by being assertive, not arrogant. Go back to your earliest memory of when you had your confidence knocked by other people and energetically transmute this negative situation into positive with the Angel Starlight energy. Ask your Guardian Angel for help in forgiving all those involved.

Success Story

Julie came to me for Angel Healing because she was feeling very low in every way. When I linked into her energy, I was told by the Angels around her that she had lost confidence in herself because some of the decisions she had made in the past had caused her problems and she no longer trusted herself or others. Her inability to make decisions was stopping her from socializing, working and even leaving home to go on long journeys. Julie then told me that she had a few failed relationships behind her and was at that point going through a divorce. Her confidence was at a real low and she had given up on life. The Angels wanted to remind her that she had been a very sociable, happy person before her broken relationships, and that this was her true, authentic self. We went through a healing and clearing exercise to remove the emotional trauma and feelings of rejection and failure so that she could move forward in her life. She didn't struggle with forgiveness and was able to let go quickly. Within days, Julie began to feel energetic and alive again, and she got back in touch with her old friends and organized a huge divorce party! Nowadays, she is very sociable and content with her life, living each day as it comes.

Stress

What is Stress?

Stress is an internal state of mind caused by an external form of energy. The main factors contributing to stress are external influences: fear, pressure, time, competition and change. The symptoms of stress can manifest on any or all levels – distress may be on an emotional level, you may feel disorientated on a mental level, suffer disease on a physical level and disconnection on a spiritual level. All these symptoms leave you feeling disempowered. Angels want to restore your peace by teaching you that you are in control every moment you choose a thought or an emotion. By adapting to your environment, which is always changing, by responding to it in a positive manner with your thoughts and practising the act of patience, you will manage to stabilize your feelings. Stress is caused when you believe that you are unable to control a situation; it makes you feel that you are a victim of circumstances. Although there may be certain things that are out of your control, only you are in control of your reactions towards them.

Stress at Work

Insecurity is the major stress factor in the workplace. Apprehension with regard to job security, financial security, status, promotion and recognition all lead to stress. Many also fear that they are not good enough, that they are being misjudged, compared to others or found to be a failure. These negative thoughts create internal stress which will affect your performance at work and will also filter through to other areas of your life. Angel Healing removes the negative thoughts and fears you hold within your mind which are the underlying causes of stress and help you to reprogramme your outlook on work. Working in an environment where you are constantly under pressure with too much to do and not enough time, constantly being made to feel that you are an under-achiever, not feeling appreciated for your efforts – all these situations result in some form of stress, and you will naturally react to your environment accordingly.

Accumulated stress may lead to exhaustion and sickness. Angels help you to respond to your environment in a positive manner. Stress cannot be healed from the outside in, it has to begin from your inner world and reflect out into your outer world. Stress is all about perception, and most of the time you may have the expectation that certain people or situations will cause you stress. For example, the first thought you may have when you wake up and make your way into work, is: 'Another stressful day ahead, I can't wait for the weekend!' As that is your expectation, your subconscious mind will be looking out for triggers through-out the day to make that your reality. Angels are able to help you to reprogramme such expectations into positive ones so that you will get the best out of each day while being at work. This will also lead to you being in control of your emotions, physical energy levels and enable you to choose your thoughts positively.

Time

One of the main stress factors in life is time. You may be faced with many short-term and long-term deadlines each day, each week, each month; this may have become a normal part of your everyday life. Because of this, it may be that, without the pressure of time, you lose enthusiasm or the motivation to achieve your deadline. If you are constantly racing against time, ask the Angels to help you manage your time effectively and work with restrictions. They will help you to become organized in the most effective way, they will clear any obstacles, allow you to delegate responsibilities to others to help ease the pressure on you, and they can magically arrange for deadline extensions. We live in such a fast-paced world and everything is happening so quickly we struggle to keep up with it all. However, the stress of time is actually a self-imposed pressure in the mind. You have the ability to prioritize what actually has to be done and what can wait. If there is an unreasonable expectation of meeting a tight deadline, you have the ability to say no and propose a different deadline, or in some cases ask for additional help. The best way to be in control of this type of stress is to take a step back and stop trying. Although there will be a fear of the consequences of not meeting the time limits in your mind, your action will bring an inner peace and will steady your nerves and calm your emotions, stop them running wild and causing havoc on your physical well-being. It is important only to do what you feel is most important; this will depend on your values. The Angels will teach you patience, which means allowing everything to happen at the right time, in the right order, in the right way. Patience doesn't mean sitting around waiting for things to happen. It is being in the very present moment rather than living in the future.

Angel Healing techniques such as meditation will take you away from the stress and illusion of not having enough time, and will help you to connect to your powerful higher consciousness which can show you a completely new perspective on your situation. Angels ask you to think about the long-term damage that stress may create on your well-being if you don't take action now to break the destructive patterns and routines in your life.

Ask the Angels to help you organize each day, and set yourself necessary and realistic deadlines. See that the top priority is always quality time for you which will restore your life-force energy; important deadlines such as meeting appointments will be second on your priority list; all minor deadlines you set yourself, such as chores, should be done at your leisure. Change the way you perceive such chores by renaming them 'choices'. It is your choice if you wish to action them or not.

Worry

Angels see that worry and anxiety unsettle your emotions and make your body restless. Worry also drains your life-force energy, leaving you feeling lethargic and slowing you down. When you add worry to something that others are worrying about, there becomes a dark grey cloud over homes, cities, countries then, eventually, the planet. As energy reacts to energy, the planet will have to respond to the build-up of negative energy being projected by humanity. It flushes this energy out in cycles through natural disasters. The Angels can remove your needless worry and guide you to take the appropriate action, which will consequently release the anxiety attached to your situation.

Conflict

Angels see arguments as battles of the ego. Opinions are beliefs which have been determined through a person's personal experience. You may never agree with the other person's outlook, so there really is no point in arguing. Angels help you to compromise through respecting others' opinions. Battles serve one purpose of empowering the ego mind (also known as lower consciousness). Beneficial arguments are those whereby you are genuinely teaching and learning from each other in order to broaden general knowledge. Ask the Angels to teach you how to listen and see things from a different perspective, honouring others' values and opinions. You may in fact be learning something through the conflict you have experienced, although your ego will disagree and want to put up a fight. When you show respect, conflict is healed and you can both go your separate ways. Angels will help you to realize that you cannot change another person, especially the person you are in a relationship with. The Angels see relationships as being about 'relating' to another, no matter what your differences are. The greatest relationships are those that challenge you through differences, because you learn about what you do not possess, be they good or bad qualities. If you possess exactly the same qualities, there is no room for growth, and this leads to stagnation and boredom. Give your frustration to the Angels so that they can help you to relate to people different from yourself without judgement.

 ## ANGEL HEALING MEDITATION FOR STRESS

ANGEL SECRET:

'Turn your distress into de-stress;
dissolve the problem by
solving it with love.'

CROWN CHAKRA

Angel Starlight enters your angelic body through a beautiful white rose just above your physical body. You see a silvery sparkling star in the centre of your crown chakra and connect with your soul. Your Guardian Angel asks you to think about the situation that is causing you stress. See that a very dark cloud is forming with all your negative thoughts within it. Feel the effect it is having on your body. Feel the tension building up in your muscles, the change in your heartbeat and the tightening, piercing stress in your stomach area. Without trying to control your thoughts in any way, just spend a few moments observing and letting them collect within the dark cloud.

THIRD-EYE CHAKRA

Angel Starlight travels down into the purple rose between your two eyes and into your mind. It now begins to clear your intuition blocks. Visualize your Guardian Angel channelling the Angel Starlight energy into your entire body through your crown chakra, transmuting the negative effects that your stressful situation is causing you on all levels. Look within your body and see the negativity being transmuted by the light, and feel the tension within your body slowly reduce until it disappears completely.

THROAT CHAKRA

Angel Starlight travels down into the blue rose in your throat and extends towards your ears. Your Guardian Angel asks you to speak about how this stress has come about in your life, what has caused it and which part of it was your responsibility. Now think about what good has come from this situation and, if you are unable to see any good coming out of it at all, ask your Guardian Angel to channel this information to you. Even if it's the smallest positive thing, it has served you in some way.

HEART CHAKRA

Angel Starlight travels down into the green rose within your heart and, as it blossoms, you see that it slowly transforms into a pink rose. Your Guardian Angel now brings your awareness to your heartbeat, which should have become more regular by this point. Keep sending Angel Starlight into this area as it continues to pump self-love around your body, also helping you to release and surrender the emotions of anger, irritability, stress, and any infuriated or unsettled feelings, so that they can also leave your body and go into the dark cloud of accumulated negative energy. Visualize your Guardian Angel now injecting the dark cloud with golden Angel Starlight that will turn the darkness into beautiful sparkling gold light. The gold light now forms into many small, sparkling stars which are returned to you and go straight into your soul. They represent the lessons you have learned through your stressful situation.

SOLAR PLEXUS CHAKRA

Angel Starlight travels down into the yellow rose within your stomach area, the core of your being. Your Guardian Angel directs more of the Angel Starlight into your solar plexus, as this is the main place within your body that residual stress accumulates. Visualize that the normally round golden sphere in the centre of your yellow rose is now completely out of shape, dark brown in colour and has harmful spikes which cause you to feel nausea as they dig into your organs. Your Guardian Angel now takes this sphere out of your body and returns it to its natural state before placing it back where it belongs. You now feel more settled and can breathe easily.

SACRAL CHAKRA

Angel Starlight travels down into the orange rose just below your navel and activates your creative abilities. You begin to feel more relaxed and grounded as you have let go of the very stressful energies which were literally attacking your body, mind, heart and soul. Thank your Guardian Angel for helping you with this healing session and ask that they strengthen and repair your

angelic body now. Visualize and feel that you are being show-
ered with the creative bright white light and that you will never
allow situations to have such an extreme negative impact on
your well-being again.

ROOT CHAKRA

Angel Starlight travels down into the red rose at the base of
your spine. Visualize your Guardian Angel sweeping all the excess
energy away from your body. You feel much lighter, as if a huge
weight has been lifted from you, and you stay in your relaxed
position until you are ready to fully awaken and face the world
again, without any traces of stress.

Success Story

Dave came to me for Angel Healing to seek relief from the stress
he was suffering. As we began the session, I was told by the Angels
that Dave needed to please others in order to feel better about
himself and, as a consequence, he took on too much responsibility at work. The same pattern was repeated in his family life: he
felt that everything lay on his shoulders, and the burdens were
creating stress in his mind and affecting his physical well-being.
During his meditation, his Guardian Angel connected with him.
It was a very peaceful experience. He was given the energy of
support and was asked to start delegating tasks or responsibilities
to others. It was brought to Dave's attention that he had a fear of
being judged by others as lazy or incapable and therefore always
tried too hard. As this baggage was lifted from him, he felt a sense
of freedom. After his session, Dave began to put himself first
much more than he would ever have done before. He started
looking after himself and spending time doing the things he
loved, rather than always giving up his time and energy for others.

Abundance

Wealth

Success is often measured by wealth. It is important to ascertain what success means to you personally and what wealth represents. Searching for wealth is usually a sign of searching for the quality that wealth brings, for example, freedom. You can be free from the moment you release fear and scarcity. Angels are able to assist you in changing your negative beliefs surrounding wealth. Traumatic phases in life are stored within the subconscious mind as negative memories, and these build up and develop over time into fears. With Angel Healing, you can heal the memories of the financial struggles you have had and the fear that these memories have created. Even if you have forgotten about your bad experiences in the past, the negative energy behind them runs as hidden programmes that influence your present moment and future.

Abundance

Abundance is a natural flow of all good things coming into your life. You are your best advertisement and you are your best manager. Angels ask you to open your mind, heart and arms so that you can break down all the barriers that are stopping you from being wealthy. The Angels guide you to connect with your power to create and to believe that you deserve abundance without guilt. They are aware of the major imbalance of abundance around the world and they wish to empower each person to use their creative abilities and make a difference to this situation. When you have dedication to serve humanity, a passion for your product and focus on using your uttermost potential, you can make a change to lives across the world on a huge scale.

Exchange

Abundance comes to you through an exchange of energy. If you are not taking responsibility for the flow in your life and are dwelling on the lack of abundance, unfortunately that is what you will continue to create. What you focus on becomes your reality, therefore if you are unable to imagine or believe that you are naturally abundant, consequently you will hold negative programmes in your subconscious mind that will influence what happens. The Angels will guide you to balance what you give and what you take so that you energetically harmonize with the law of karma. This means that whatever you give out comes back to you. The more generous you are with giving some form of energy, the more you will generate opportunities to receive some form of energy. The most influential form of energy in our era is financial exchange, therefore the logical mind may struggle with the concept 'The more I give, the more I get back.' On an energetic level, by giving to others, you are sending out many positive signals of being abundant and wealthy enough to be able to freely give. This opens the channels for you to openly and willingly receive from other sources and gives you a sense of being worthy and deserving of abundance without feeling guilty.

Deserving and Allowing

Even though you may consciously be praying for abundance to come into your life, you may have been subconsciously blocking it. To create a natural flow of abundance in your life, you have to build a good relationship with energy. By changing the way you view your outgoing bills and expenses, you will project a different energy into your concept of financial abundance. If you give gratitude for the services your utility bills have provided you, then you will lovingly pay. When you pay with love, you receive with love. If you begin to think how, when and why you should receive abundance, you immediately sabotage the blessings that are rightfully yours with negative thinking patterns. Angels will bring it to your attention each time you have a negative or limited belief, and they ask that you open your arms and patiently wait for miracles with unwavering faith.

ANGEL HEALING MEDITATION FOR ABUNDANCE

ANGEL SECRET:

'What you appreciate appreciates in value.'

CROWN CHAKRA

Angel Starlight enters your angelic body through a beautiful white rose just above your physical body. You see a silvery sparkling star in the centre of your crown chakra and connect with your soul. Your Guardian Angel now expands your consciousness to connect with the universal laws. As you shift your awareness from the logical and limited mind to the expansive higher consciousness of all possibilities, you prepare to go on a journey to find your true abundance in life.

THIRD-EYE CHAKRA

Angel Starlight travels down into the purple rose between your two eyes and into your mind. It now begins to clear your intuition blocks. Your Guardian Angel asks you how you would feel if you were left with nothing but the clothes you are wearing, food and water to last you a lifetime and a shelter over your head. Visualize what this would mean to your identity and status. Now that you have the opportunity to show your true potential and create an abundance, what would you want an abundance of, and why? How would an abundance of that quality change your life?

THROAT CHAKRA

Angel Starlight travels down into the blue rose in your throat and extends towards your ears. Your Guardian Angel asks you to determine your highest values in life. Think about what is most important to you and if you were living the perfect life, where would you be, who would you be there with and what would you be doing. Now speak about why you are not there, living your ideal life. After speaking about this, visualize your Guardian Angel completely erasing these thoughts from your memory and transmuting the reason why you believe you cannot fulfil your dreams into knowing that you can.

HEART CHAKRA

Angel Starlight travels down into the green rose within your heart and, as it blossoms, you see that it slowly transforms into a pink rose. Your Guardian Angel asks you to feel the love in your heart for life. What is missing in your life right now, and why do you not have it? Which fears are holding you back from achieving this state of abundance? Have you truly followed your heart to achieve all your desires in life, or have others' opinions or rules stopped you from following your heart? As you answer your Guardian Angels questions, you completely release all your fears about following your heart.

SOLAR PLEXUS CHAKRA

Angel Starlight travels down into the yellow rose within your stomach area, the core of your being. Your Guardian Angel directs the Angel Starlight to your fears of survival, security, status, detachment, of not being accepted and not being loved. Ask yourself if you have a fear of failure or a fear of success, or both simultaneously. Ask that your Guardian Angel changes your fears into self-belief and to ensure that you are completely capable of succeeding and accepting your spiritual rewards.

SACRAL CHAKRA

Angel Starlight travels down into the orange rose just below your navel and activates your creative abilities. Your Guardian Angel now asks you to use your creative imagination to imagine how you can change your life to have all that you want by using your creative abilities, skills and talents. What are the qualities that you want in your life? Visualize that you have all of these qualities and you have the power to spread abundance to all those in need around the world.

ROOT CHAKRA

Angel Starlight travels down into the red rose at the base of your spine. You are now completely attuned with the universal laws, which are teaching you that you can be abundant, especially with the help of your Guardian Angel. You now have a constant flow of abundance in the form you need it. Through the law of karma, the more you give, the more you receive. By means of the law of attraction, your outer world is reflected by your inner world. Through the law of gratitude, what you appreciate and give many thanks for multiplies tenfold. Repeat the affirmation: 'Angel Starlight brings me plenty of all that I desire.'

Success Story

Sandy had Angel Healing because he wanted to create financial abundance in his life while doing the work he loves the most. While doing a reading for him, I was shown by the Angels that he had been extremely disappointed by others he had worked with in the past, and this had led to him not being able to trust others. Sandy agreed that this was true and told me that he had been a very successful entrepreneur and had had no financial worries. However, he had made the wrong decision on an investment and had also been taken advantage of by his business partner, which resulted in a huge financial loss. Naturally, this ruined his confidence and self-esteem, so moving forward from this situation was a big challenge. Sandy had always believed in the power of prayer and had never given up. During his meditation, he connected with Archangel Michael's energy, to free him from his guilt, regrets and anger about the past and to enable him to take his power back. As he released the negativity from within his emotional and energetic body, he got back in touch with his creative energy. His life was completely transformed from hopelessness and despair to success and happiness. His circle of friends changed, as he began attracting like-minded, positive people, and wonderful opportunities started to come his way. Sandy mastered the art of attracting abundance by asking the Angels daily to guide him towards prosperity and to make the business he is passionate about flourish.

Practical Exercises with
Archangel Gabriel
(Channelling Creative Writing
for Healing the Mind)

Positive Thinking

It is time to examine whether you are in control of your mind, or if your mind is in control of your life. Divide your life into important areas such as love and relationships, wealth and prosperity, career and life purpose, health and well-being. Under each section, write a list of negative beliefs you hold within your mind, then write down the positive element that you would prefer to believe. Once they have all been written, think about the origins of the negative belief – what age were you? At what phase of your life? Which person or situation had an influence in creating it? – and ask that the memory is removed from your consciousness. For each statement, reprogramme your mind by saying, 'With my will and intention, I choose to change the following belief (negative statement) into (positive statement).' Do this exercise whenever you hear yourself speaking, feeling and thinking in an unloving way towards yourself, your life or towards others.

Overcoming Fears

Your fears have been holding you back from experiencing life at its best and at your fullest capacity. Write down a list of all your physical fears (for example, fear of heights), psychological fears (for example, fear of failure), emotional fears (for example, fear of rejection) and spiritual fears (fear of not fulfilling your life purpose). When you feel ready to confront and heal them, in your own time and in any order that you wish, work on them individually by finding a quiet place where you are in a relaxed environment. Close your eyes for a few moments and, when you are ready to write, open your eyes and allow your memories, thoughts and feelings to flow through your body on to paper. Begin by writing, 'At the age of ...', 'When I was ...', and tell your story so that you can rationalize your fears. Your writing will naturally come to an end when you have understood the fear, and you will be able to release it from your mind fully.

Having a Successful Career

Do not allow your career to dictate your identity; let your identity reflect through your career. Review your current situation by answering the following questions: Are you doing the work you love? If not, what would you love to do if you could? Have you taken any action to achieve this? If not, why not? What are the fears that are holding you back? Are you willing to take a risk? If not, what have you got to lose? Write a list of what is most important to you regarding your career, prioritizing from highest to lowest. Some examples may be financial rewards, emotionally fulfilment, mental and creative stimulus, physical comfort and spiritual satisfaction. Have clarity about what success means to you and how you can achieve success through your career. Ask for angelic guidance to find a career that suits your values, priorities and requirements. If you are unable to change your career, ask that you can reshape your current role in order to fulfil all your desires.

Creativity

Tap into your creative energy by imagining your life as though you already have achieved everything you set out to create. As you picture it in your mind, feel the emotions that you will have in your heart and feel them running through your whole body. This technique will awaken your natural creative abilities to transform everything that is not working in your life to making it work exactly how it should. Each morning, make a wish list of what you wish to create, whether it is a whole day of peace, a certain amount of clients, to complete tasks in a timely manner or to create miraculous outcomes to difficult situations. At the end of each day, look back at your list and tick off what you have achieved. For those that you have not achieved, ask yourself what action you could have taken to make this happen, but most importantly, review your beliefs around being able to achieve it. Do you feel that you deserve to have it? Do you feel that you are worthy of having it? While working on creative projects, always see the end successful result, rather than worrying how it's going to be achieved, as this will ensure you fulfil your highest creative potential.

Confidence

The best way to have true inner confidence is to believe in yourself. To believe in yourself fully, you have to know yourself fully. Connect with your body, mind, heart and soul by taking a few moments each day to look into a mirror and observe, not criticize. The most important questions to ask are 'What is it that needs to change' and 'Why do you want it to change?' Do not worry about how, where or when. Allow the miraculous healing qualities of the Angels to guide and empower you to achieve the changes. All you need to focus on is the pure intention and reason for change, and ultimately this will lead to confidence when you do achieve your desired result. In the meantime, focus on your achievements rather than your failures and the good qualities that your loved ones see within you. Knowledge and experience is confidence. Talk about and embrace the subjects you know most about, while learning and developing your general knowledge and in weaker areas. Looking confident will make you feel confident and, eventually, you will be naturally confident.

Stress

When stress is inflicted upon you, it causes you to be out of synch with the natural flow of life. To combat this build-up of negative energy, burn incense and wave the smoke around your aura, concentrating on each chakra, especially the solar plexus, as stress is held in the stomach. Cleanse your room by opening the windows and clear up any clutter which may be blocking the universal energy from flowing through. Use water to cleanse the negative energy of stress in your inner body and outer body. Wash your hands and face, or have a shower, to wash away all traces of negativity and flush out all the toxins within you. Take a few deep breaths of fresh air, hold, and release slowly. Repeat the affirmation: 'I am cool, calm and collected' for as long as you need. Light a white candle and hold an intention that all stress within the world is melting away as the candle burns.

Abundance

What does abundance mean to you? If your answer is wealth, rather than focusing on financial reward, focus on the physical, mental, emotional and spiritual rewards that financial gain will bring into your life. Write down all the qualities which you believe having a huge abundance of wealth can buy, such as freedom, security, happiness and comfort. Your logical mind is limited to believing that these qualities will only come to you through material gain and possessions. Your infinite and boundless mind will teach you other ways of living these qualities when you allow the creative inspirations and ideas to flow into your life. Each day, even if it feels like a pretence, make an effort to live your life by expressing qualities such as freedom and security. Eventually they will become deeply embedded within your subconscious mind and become your reality. One of the magical ways that this works is by Angels guiding certain people into your life through whom you can provide exchanges of service, knowledge and opportunities without the need for financial exchange.

PART VII:

ANGEL HEALING
FOR THE HEART

This section will cover the main emotional challenges people face throughout their lives, with particular emphasis on love relationships. There will be a short description of the problem and how it is usually caused. The advice has been directly channelled from the Angels, providing a completely different perspective on the situation. After each section, there is an Angel Healing meditation, which will begin to release any blocks you may have in this area on an energetic level. The practical exercises provide ideas of action to be taken, and affirmations for the mind will enhance your healing as they change your thought patterns into positivity.

All emotions are expressions of the two powerful emotions: love or fear. A positive emotion is love; a negative one, fear. Where there is love, there is no fear. Love and fear cannot be expressed at the same time. Love is light and fear is dark, so fear disappears when the light of love is switched on. All variations of the emotion love, such as peace, joy and happiness, already exist within you. Through various life experiences, they may lose their existence to fear, which creates negative emotions, such as anger, sadness or guilt. Angel Healing will help you understand your emotions and transform fear back into love, your negative emotion into a positive emotion. In life, there is a constant movement between these types of emotions, however, when you make an effort to take control of your emotional well-being, you will know how to identify and transform your emotions from negative into positive. Expecting to be emotionally happy and positive all the time is unreasonable, and also unhealthy. Being balanced means being at peace. When you recognize a negative emotion, you can change it. Negative emotions have a negative effect on the aura and chakras, which remain in certain areas of the physical body. This leads to low energy, which then leads to ill health or disease. Emotions are not reprogrammed within the mind, like thoughts and beliefs. They are energies which change in frequency according to the influence of thoughts and external factors. Emotions have an impact on all relationships with other people, with yourself and with life itself, therefore, the healthier and more positive your emotions are, the more healthily and positively your relationships will flow.

The Angels' definition of love is natural perfection. They say that this energy exists within everything, everyone and everywhere. Love is an infinite, expanding energy which cannot be destroyed, only tainted. Everything has an energetic frequency, and by changing your own energy and inner world to the frequency of love, you will be attracting love in all forms, whether it is via relationships with people or attracting the work you love to do. With dedication and practice, you will be able to resonate with the frequency of love in every experience you have, whether internally or externally. Guardian Angels will guide you to remember the pure feeling of love and to feel it in every moment of your life.

In Angel Healing, the goal is to replace whatever has contaminated the purity of love and to return it to its natural state of existence. This is done when the Angels channel their own energy of love (which we call Angel Starlight) into the situation to transmute the negative energy around it, to return it to natural perfection. Although many people search for love externally, through everything that they do, in their search for potential partners, in their careers or passions, the Angels remind us that love will not be found externally, as it already resides within you and can only be expressed from within. When love is blocked physically, mentally, emotionally and spiritually, the person loses touch with their natural joy, wisdom, health and peace and becomes doubtful that they will ever find true happiness within themselves so they begin searching for it externally. The secret is to use the Angels' guidance and healing energy in order to find love from within and to let it shine through into every area of your life.

Love is the highest form of energy. Energy vibrates at different frequencies, and as love is the highest form of energy known to humanity, it is a great healer. Calling upon your Guardian Angel and the Archangels to teach you about love will open up many doors and opportunities for you to experience love in all its forms. The most potent way of experiencing love in its purest form is in your relationships towards children. This is because young children carry the innocence, purity and essence of love, as they have not been influenced by life experience. They radiate love and therefore effortlessly attract love back. These young souls absorb everything into their subconscious mind, and this will have a strong influence on how much they will express or suppress love as they grow older.

Once you become conscious of how much love you have towards yourself, towards others, your life and the world, you take control of your happiness and fulfilment. As the energy of love is magnetic, the more you learn to love yourself, the more you will be loved by others. Energies have a way of communicating with each other, so whatever you do not love about yourself will be brought to your attention until you do something about it – like heal it! This is why patterns form, for example of attracting certain types of people or situations into your life.

Once you are true to yourself and acknowledge the negative blocks within you, you allow change and healing to occur. Love is endless and doesn't require an exchange. The more you give love, the more you will naturally receive, as there is an infinite abundance of love in the universe. Not enough people are tapping into this energy because they have been influenced in a negative way by the ego mind. Love is an unconditional state of being when used in the most authentic way. Conditions placed on love ruin its purity and create unhealthy attachments and expectations. These come from a place of fear. Love creates miracles and can heal all wounds, on physical, mental, emotional and spiritual levels. Love is the most beautiful and incredible emotion that exists. Disappointment occurs when our love is not appreciated, and sorrow comes from lack of love. Forgiveness brings us back to love. Grief is the pain of losing love, and patience comes from trusting love. As we reawaken to love, we become enlightened beings who believe in their highest potential. Love has the power to dissolve negativity and helps to create love and peace all around the world.

Relationships are an important factor in teaching you about yourself, getting to understand the person you really are. It has nothing much to do with the other person at all. What you like, dislike and the way you live your life are determined by your soul awareness and your values. By sharing your life with others through relationships, whether with your partner, your child or your colleagues, you are seeing how compatible you are.

Those who you call soul mates have a similar soul aware-ness; you have a connection beyond your personality. You are unable to describe or rationalize this connection, because it is so deep. Relationships require both parties to compromise on val-ues and, depending on how stubborn each individual is about changing, this determines the amount of challenges. Unless one partner backs down and gets on with things, there will be clashes. Clashes are conflict and lead to unhappiness. This is the case in all relationships: love, work, family, etc. The secret to a happy relationship is communication and understanding through angelic wisdom, and respect and compassion through angelic love. You cannot change another person, however, you can inspire the other person to change. There is a huge difference between the two, and with Angel Healing you can see the other person through Angel's eyes. There will be no need for forgive-ness if you have no expectations of the other person in the first place. In order to have no expectations, apart from decency and respect for one another, you must completely love yourself, accept your strengths and weaknesses and believe in your values. Unless you do this, you will be unable to sustain a long-term healthy relationship with another person. When you are com-pletely happy, fulfilled and content with yourself, you can unconditionally love yourself for who you are. This way, the feeling of loneliness dissolves, as there is nothing missing in you or your life.

However, wanting to share your life with a special person, to enjoy the good times and grow from bad times is different. If you are happy, fulfilled and content with yourself, it reduces the pressure placed upon the other person to fulfil you and there is a sense of appreciation for every moment you spend together. The best relationships are those where you don't feel emptiness when they are not around but you feel like it's the first time you've met when you do see each other. It's a feeling of independent togetherness. It is important to express your feelings and true thoughts about yourself and to be able to listen to another person's perspective.

Each person you meet and have a loving connection with has a gift for you. Even if the situation is challenging or hurtful at the time, there will always be a higher purpose or reason and something to learn. Those with whom you have very special connections are members of your soul group, your soul mates, and they will teach you the biggest lessons for your soul's growth.

Loneliness

No Relationship

You feel alone. Angels hear your request for wanting to be in a relationship and want to say that in order to find what is missing in your life, first you must take a review of the way you love yourself and look at those aspects of yourself that you are not accepting within. Are you absolutely ready to love another person by being in a relationship? Are you absolutely ready to be loved for exactly who you are? If you do not love parts of yourself, it will be very difficult for another person to love them. Your heart's desire is to express love. It searches for another heart which also understands love. People have a perception that the only way to express love is in a special relationship with a significant other. It's time to change this perception and to understand that, as everyone is looking to express love and feel that they belong, it's time to open your hearts to each other. This will remove your feelings of loneliness physically and emotionally. Sharing love through your heart will naturally attract many people to you. Longing for a relationship to cover your feelings of loneliness is unhealthy. Coming together with another heart through fear of always being alone is a temporary fix and does not lead to permanent fulfilment or satisfaction, as you will not find the answers to the root cause of your loneliness. The best relationship you can have is with yourself.

Separation

Loneliness can lead to feelings of deep unhappiness and unworthiness. Loneliness can be described as feeling completely isolated and having a huge void within you. Angels understand that when a relationship comes to an end, it may completely change your life. You feel as though something major is missing. Your physical world no longer seems full and you have more time to dwell on what is missing. The feeling of loneliness is caused when there is a separation between your body, mind, heart and soul. Whichever link is missing, it creates a disconnection. People search to restore this connection outside of themselves and expect to alleviate loneliness through a connection with another person or people. Your Guardian Angel is always with you, providing all the love, comfort and everything else that your heart might need. Once you start opening up and feeling your Guardian Angel around you, the sense of loneliness will completely disappear.

Company

Angels say that when you love yourself and your own company, others will love you and your company in the same way. When you become comfortable in your own internal spaces of your mind, heart and body, you will naturally start radiating peace through into your external world and the feeling of needing a relationship, or something to fill your emptiness, will dissolve. Always remember you will always attract into your life what you have within you.

Friendships

If you are looking for a relationship with someone special to be together with physically, you must change your focus from what is lacking in your life to what you deserve to have in your life. When you make a change in your thoughts, your feelings will also change and so will the energy vibrations you radiate out into the world. In time, your actions will be driven from a more positive perspective. No one is truly alone when they begin to appreciate the people they already have in their lives. Angels ask you to think about whether you make enough effort to stay in touch with friends with whom you may have lost touch. Angels will give you the courage to make steps to meet new people by joining social groups so that you can meet people who share a common interest.

Independence

Ask the Angels to guide you towards becoming an independent and fulfilled person now. They will radiate a very attractive and inspirational energy through you which will attract others into your life. Show the world who you really are, rather than who you think you should be, and people will acknowledge you more. Feel ready, open, willing and fearless to allow someone close to your heart and they will appear naturally. When you have the perfect relationship with yourself, you will have the perfect relationship with others.

ANGEL HEALING MEDITATION FOR LONELINESS

ANGEL SECRET:

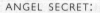

'Loneliness is void when you believe in oneness, as oneness is within loneliness.'

CROWN CHAKRA

Angel Starlight enters your angelic body through a beautiful white rose just above your physical body. You see a silvery sparkling star in the centre of your crown chakra and connect with your soul. It may take a while to find this star; be patient, and you'll know when the connection has been made. The golden Angel Starlight is brightening your soul, awakening your angelic wisdom. Ask your soul now to show you what loneliness is and how it relates to your life. As the rays of your soul shine out into the world, you now connect with all souls which are all part of the oneness in the universe.

THIRD-EYE CHAKRA

Angel Starlight travels down into the purple rose between your two eyes and into your mind. It now begins to clear any blocks to your intuition. Your Guardian Angel takes you on a journey into your past to show you how much unhappiness the feeling of loneliness has caused you. As you live through these phases of your life, your Guardian Angel directs the golden Angel Starlight to transmute your bad memories into love, and you see them dissolving them into golden light. Visualize yourself taking the wisdom from these experiences and placing them into your purple rose.

THROAT CHAKRA

Angel Starlight travels down into the blue rose in your throat and extends towards your ears. Your Guardian Angel asks you to speak about your feelings of loneliness, either out loud or within your mind. As you communicate, you see that the blue rose becomes more vibrant in colour and opens up fully. Trust and allow everything that has been stuck in this area to flow out, as this is a way of releasing negative thoughts. Listen to your Guardian Angel's perspective on loneliness and their advice about the next steps you must take in your life to find what seems to be missing.

HEART CHAKRA

Angel Starlight travels down into the green rose within your heart and, as it blossoms, you see that it slowly transforms into a pink rose. Your Guardian Angel sends the energy of strength into your heart and fills the emptiness with pure unconditional love. Visualize the pink rose expanding into a beautiful heartshape as large as your physical body, merging you even closer with your Guardian Angel so that you become one. You will never feel loneliness again, as you now have the ability to connect with people, Angels and situations through your expansive heart, even if they are not around you physically.

SOLAR PLEXUS CHAKRA

Angel Starlight travels down into the yellow rose within your stomach area, the core of your being. Your Guardian Angel now channels the energy of power into this area until you find your true identity as an independent and confident person. Feel the Angel Starlight now healing your insecurities and giving you the knowledge that you deserve to be appreciated for who you are. Visualize that within your yellow rose, there is a dark spot. This represents your fear of being alone. This spot is now being washed away with Angel Starlight as you repeat the affirmation: 'I am surrounded by love.'

SACRAL CHAKRA

Angel Starlight travels down into the orange rose just below your navel and activates your creative abilities. Your Guardian Angel helps you to find within this area the pattern of loneliness and shows you how it has followed you throughout your whole life. The Angel Starlight is now breaking that pattern and is giving you the energy of freedom. Feel it running through your body. You now heal any resentment towards those who may have ended relationships with you and caused you feelings of loneliness. Visualize that beautiful cords of love now attach to your special loved ones and to everyone who will very soon be coming into your life. See the golden Angel Starlight flowing through these cords, strengthening your bond with unconditional love.

ROOT CHAKRA

Angel Starlight travels down into the red rose at the base of your spine. Look very deep within this red rose as your Guardian Angel takes you on a long journey back to your childhood. Think about whether or not, as a child, you felt as though you belonged in this world. Did you fit in with other groups, or did you always feel left out? Did you have many friends, or did you play on your own? Your Guardian Angel is now directing the Angel Starlight to transmute all negative memories, beliefs and situations during your childhood and erasing them from your memory. It is healing all the traumas you may have experienced or witnessed as a child that led you to feel alone. As you witness this healing, watch yourself grow from being a child into your present moment, knowing that all the times you have felt lonely in your life have been erased from your memory and replaced with self-love and independence. Repeat the affirmation: 'Angel Starlight has now healed my loneliness.'

Success Story

Ebony came to Angel Healing to alleviate her loneliness; she did not feel fulfilled in her life. In her meditation, she was taken on a journey away from her physical reality and shown that she had many Angels and spirit guides around her who were trying to bring guidance in enabling her to expand her social group. Ebony had left her corporate job in the City of London and decided to work from home as a financial trader. She did this for four years and, having removed herself from the business and social network, she came to feel very isolated. She was fearful that she no longer had anything in common with the outside world. The healing energy gradually gave her the direction to leave her comfort zone and pursue a change in her career. She was not enjoying it and it was no longer profitable. Ebony was given counselling and life coaching from her Angels to enable her to understand what it was that was holding her back from moving forward. Within a few weeks, she followed the guidance she had been given and went for some job interviews in the City. Within a month or two, she had found a new job, and now she is very happy, with a great new circle of friends.

Rejection

Unreciprocated Love

The feeling of rejection comes in many forms. It is a feeling that you have chosen to have because another person has made a decision that did not suit your needs. Angels know how tormenting being in love with someone who is unavailable or does not love you back is. You take it very personally and start feeling unworthy or not good enough, and this has a very negative impact on your self-esteem. This feeling starts the process of looking within and finding what it is you are rejecting about yourself; then you can begin the process of becoming empowered to change. Angels ask that you find the strength from loving yourself without doubting that you deserve this love. Believe that relationships are your divine right and that you deserve to be in the best one for you. Never put up with coming in second place. Angels say that when you give up trying or chasing the person, they will start chasing you! If you are truly meant to be together, you will come together when you let go of all unhealthy attachments.

Self-Development

Angels say that if the person you love and want to be with is in a relationship with another person, the natural reaction is to compare yourself to them, looking at what they have got that you have not. Without allowing yourself negative feelings of jealousy or envy towards the other person, see it as a good opportunity for you to look within and find what you think is missing within you. If you are determined to heal your feelings of rejection, Angels will lead you on to a self-development path and will play a big part in your growth. They will guide you to divert your focus from wanting what you haven't got to knowing that you have all that you want.

Healing the Past

Angels believe that the trauma caused by rejection creates a negative belief that this is what will always happen in the future. You start believing that you are not worthy of love or attention, and this turns into negative emotions of low self-worth. Negative beliefs such as 'I will always be rejected by those that I love' will create a recurring pattern in your relationships unless they are reprogrammed into positive programmes in your subconscious mind such as 'I deserve to be accepted.' Angels help you to look back into your past, all the way back into your childhood, to identify the root cause of your beliefs about rejection. They may stem from not receiving enough attention or being abandoned by a parent as a child. When you release the resentment towards people who have rejected you, you will be empowered

Challenge

There may be hidden reasons why you may feel attracted to people who are unavailable, and this state of affairs may be serving you on some level. For instance, it could be that you actually have a fear of commitment, or fear that being too attached to another person will cause you to lose your independence. However, a part of you really does want to be in a relationship, so there is an inner battle going on. Falling in love with someone you know you will not be able to be with gives you hope, the hope that one day he or she will fall in love with you too. It gives you drive and a purpose for living, something to focus on. Wanting to be with someone who is unattainable brings challenge and sets you a goal that your heart is trying to achieve.

Fear

The fear of being rejected will stop you from pursuing a relationship with the one you love, especially when you do not know how the person you love feels about you. This causes frustration and insecurity about yourself and will hold you back from moving forward towards happiness. Angel Healing can give you the confidence to confront this fear and to connect to the other person on a soul level to find out how they actually feel. It could even be that you are mirroring each other's fears and missing out on sharing love. Angels will help you to change your fears about rejection so that you will become more confident and naturally attractive.

ANGEL HEALING MEDITATION FOR REJECTION

ANGEL SECRET:

'Rejection cannot happen when you bless everyone for their choices.'

CROWN CHAKRA

Angel Starlight enters your angelic body through a beautiful white rose just above your physical body. You see a silvery sparkling star in the centre of your crown chakra and connect with your soul. Your Guardian Angel knows the real reason why you have been rejected in certain situations and will now show you why they happened. Be patient as you come to understand on a soul level what your lesson was in this situation, what you have learned in order to grow and what gift the person who has rejected you has given you.

THIRD-EYE CHAKRA

Angel Starlight travels down into the purple rose between your two eyes and into your mind. It now begins to clear your intuition blocks. Your Guardian Angel helps you to see how you and the person involved are on different energetic frequency levels physically, mentally, emotionally or spiritually. You will also realize why you are not compatible with each other. The Angel Starlight energy clears away your negative feelings so that you can be inspired to change your life for the better.

THROAT CHAKRA

Angel Starlight travels down into the blue rose in your throat and extends towards your ears. Your Guardian Angel now asks you to communicate your feelings of being rejected out loud or telepathically. Ask about the steps you need to take to continue your healing journey and see that your Guardian Angel places a blue energy of protection around you to keep you safe. Listen to your Guardian Angel's advice as they build your self-esteem and confidence to move forward in your life. If you feel guided to communicate with the other person involved, ask that the Angel Starlight energy runs through you so that you can be positive and express yourself clearly.

HEART CHAKRA

Angel Starlight travels down into the green rose within your heart and, as it blossoms, you see that it slowly transforms into a pink rose. Your Guardian Angel takes away the negative feelings of embarrassment, unworthiness, jealousy or envy from within you. Feel that these energies are being transmuted into compassion and given back to you as self-esteem. This energy is now flowing through your heart, melting away the unhealthy attachments you have towards the person and setting you free.

SOLAR PLEXUS CHAKRA

Angel Starlight travels down into the yellow rose within your stomach area, the core of your being. Your Guardian Angel locates the negative cords creating power struggles between you and other people. You now realize that the person who has rejected you may have done so to boost their own confidence or self-esteem, and your Guardian Angel dissolves these dark cords so that you can become empowered. From this moment onwards, people will react to the way you feel about yourself and, if you are powerful, the effects of rejection will no longer exist.

SACRAL CHAKRA

Angel Starlight travels down into the orange rose just below your navel and activates your creative abilities. Your Guardian Angel now measures your confidence levels. On a scale of 1 to 10, 10 being the most confident, visualize and feel the frequency level of your confidence. Ask your Guardian Angel what emotion or quality is needed within you in order to raise the energetic frequency to a 10. Visualize the Angel Starlight providing the energy of what you need and continue doing this until you see the scale move to a 10.

ROOT CHAKRA

Angel Starlight travels down into the red rose at the base of your spine. Look very deep within this red rose as your Guardian Angel takes you on a long journey back into your past, year by year remembering all the times you have felt rejected by others in all areas of your life. As you regress back with your Guardian Angel by your side, direct the Angel Starlight into these negative memories and watch as they are transmuted into happy memories only. As you see this healing happening, watch yourself grow from being a child into your present moment, knowing that all the times that you have felt rejected in your life have been erased from your memory and replaced with self-acceptance. Repeat the affirmation: 'Angel Starlight has now healed my rejection.'

Success Story

I experienced rejection in my life from many people when I was growing up. I never seemed to fit into the crowd, because I didn't really have much to say. It was a horrible feeling and left me feeling very demoralized. As I grew older, I had the same feeling when I was rejected by companies I had applied to for work. Later, I remember begging my Angels night and day to be accepted by a certain company I thought would be perfect for me. When my application was rejected, I felt worthless, and I couldn't understand it, because I had given my all at the interview and had all the skills and qualifications they were looking for. I was devastated, but continued searching for work elsewhere. I ended up finding a job in a much larger organization that offered a better reward package, and there I met life-long friends. About six months or so later, I heard that the company I had been so desperate to work for had closed down due to bankruptcy. At that point, I understood the hidden blessing behind my being rejected, and understood from my Angels that I should trust that my prayers are always heard, and that, if they are not answered, there is a reason for it.

Bullying

Abuse

Abuse can be directly or indirectly inflicted upon you, in any form. Whether it is on a physical, mental or emotional level, bullying is always awful and will have a severe effect on your well-being. Examples of bullying are humiliation, assault, threats, isolation, knocking confidence and taking your freedom, dignity or power away.

Victims

Angels believe that bullying is a projection of one person's unhappiness into another person's life. The person inflicting this energy, the bully, is in no way a happy, secure or peaceful person, and they also need healing, maybe more than the victim. People who are happy and at peace do not feel the need to take another person's happiness away, as it is not a natural human instinct to do so. At the same time, those who are completely secure do not feel the need to make another feel insecure. Bullies have usually been victims themselves at some point, and the only way for them to take revenge, to work out their resentment or anger, is to project these feelings on others, especially those closest to them. This makes them feel as if they are taking their power back.

Weakness

Angels see that there are weaknesses in both parties, but for different reasons, and that each party has attracted the other into their life in order to find their strengths. The bully is trying to hide their own weaknesses and insecurities by putting on an act and pretending that they are stronger than the victim. The victim will believe that they are weak because they are being overpowered by negative energy.

Jealousy

Someone may also become a bully because are they are jealous, envious or feel threatened by you, believe it or not. Angels will help you to find what it is they are jealous of, but more than likely the answer is that they feel the sense of happiness, peace and security you have within you is lacking within them. Their aim is to take this away from you by making you feel inadequate and not worthy. Many bullies may not even be aware that they are affecting people in this way, as they can only give out what they have within themselves subconsciously. You are not responsible for their life – you can only work on yourself and, as you change, the way they behave towards you will change too. That doesn't mean that you need to appear unhappy in order for them to give up, it means that you need to find compassion in your heart towards them and their actions. Negative energy from both ends creates chaos. When one person (usually the victim) doesn't react to the negativity and remains in a place of love and peace, the negativity is healed.

Stress

Angels do not want to make excuses for bullying, however they say that stress plays a huge factor in people's behaviour, especially in the workplace. People experience stress as lack of peace, caused because an external pressure has been placed upon them. The projection of stress towards others may appear to be bullying or abuse. Although stress is not an excuse for attacking another, it is an important factor to bear in mind when identifying what is creating the situation before you can start the healing process. Angels want you to believe that you are in control of your external world. Although you have no power to change the other person, you may be able to help them to cope with stress. People will then react differently towards you.

Control

Angels know that people need to feel powerful and project this out into the world for their own survival. This means that when someone feels insecure, they behave in a way to make you feel insecure too. When you are in control of your emotions, people will react towards to you more positively. Take action to show you are not putting up with bullying by taking the control of your life back. Angels will help you to face the fears that have held you back from dealing with the bullying, so that you can feel liberated.

ANGEL HEALING MEDITATION FOR BULLYING

ANGEL SECRET:

'True power is teaching unconditional love by being the perfect example.'

CROWN CHAKRA

Angel Starlight enters your angelic body through a beautiful white rose just above your physical body. You see a silvery sparkling star in the centre of your crown chakra and connect with your soul. Your Guardian Angel is now cleansing and purifying each and every part of you with the Angel Starlight energy. You feel re-energized and ready to confront your situation with the wisdom of your soul, the guidance of your Guardian Angel and the protection of the Archangels. You will be guided to take each small or large step in perfect divine timing.

THIRD-EYE CHAKRA

Angel Starlight travels down into the purple rose between your two eyes and into your mind. It now begins to clear any blocks on your intuition. Your Guardian Angel shows you that you have become a new, confident, strong and powerful person. See yourself taking the appropriate action in the situation you are faced with. You believe in your intuition and that you will be guided to take the steps that will lead to your highest and best good. Any fear or apprehension is washed away with the Angel Starlight. See this bright energy transforming the emotion of fear into love.

THROAT CHAKRA

Angel Starlight travels down into the blue rose in your throat and extends towards your ears. Your Guardian Angel asks you to communicate your feelings about your experience of being bullied either out loud or in your mind. Feel that you are releasing everything that you have bottled up within you for many years which may have been too difficult to confront. Your Guardian Angel now comforts you and wipes away the darkness from your throat chakra, promising to help you move forward now that you have asked for angelic assistance.

HEART CHAKRA

Angel Starlight travels down into the green rose within your heart and, as it blossoms, you see that it slowly transforms into a pink rose. Your Guardian Angel now shows you how frail your heart has become through the bullying and abuse it has endured. Feel that the dark-pink rose is now being watered by the Angel Starlight, bringing it back to life. Watch as it blossoms into a vibrant green and pink rose and believe that it is now preparing to forgive all those who have hurt you in any way.

SOLAR PLEXUS CHAKRA

Angel Starlight travels down into the yellow rose within your stomach area, the core of your being. Your Guardian Angel is now unfolding and removing all the dark layers around your golden core. Angel Starlight washes away the negativity until you connect with your inner power. Watch as it grows larger and larger as you start affirming to yourself: 'I am powerful,' repeating it throughout the rest of this exercise and each night as you fall asleep.

SACRAL CHAKRA

Angel Starlight travels down into the orange rose just below your navel and activates your creative abilities. Your Guardian

Angel now takes you back to your first ever relationship. Look into the dynamics of this relationship, how powerful you felt about your role and how you were treated. Were you expressing yourself fully, or were you holding a lot of yourself back? If there was any form of abuse or bullying, visualize the Angel Starlight transmuting the negative memories and see yourself undoing the actions of your partner as though they never happened. Put it all down to experience and life lessons which are part of your learning journey.

ROOT CHAKRA

Angel Starlight travels down into the red rose at the base of your spine. Look very deep within this red rose as your Guardian Angel takes you on a long journey back to your childhood. How were you treated by parents, family and fellow schoolchildren? As you remember the memories, certain people and situations may come into your mind. See yourself handing all the dark, negative emotions of anger, resentment, hatred, guilt, embarrassment, etc., to your Guardian Angel. These emotions are now being dissolved by the bright, powerful Angel Starlight, and you feel ready to confront your current situation to end the bullying and the negative effects it has had on you once and for all. Repeat the affirmation: 'Angel Starlight has now removed all negative effects of bullying.'

Success Story

Emma sought out Angel Healing because she had been suffering verbal and emotional abuse in her workplace for many years. Her colleagues treated her very differently to anybody else and excluded her from meetings and social events. She described feeling as if she was an invisible slave. During her healing meditation, she was asked to think back to her previous jobs, to her education and to when she was a child, to see if this same feeling had manifested itself in the past. She had completely forgotten that she had indeed felt invisible most of her life. The healing energy went back into her past and she began to release all the hurtful emotions about not being worthy or good enough to be acknowledged. The Angels showed her that people always react to others' vibes and actions. Without being aware of it, Emma had been subconsciously sending out the signals of being a victim rather than a confident grown woman who believed in herself. The Angels had asked her to step into a third person's position and to review her body language and behaviour in the office. This immediately prompted Emma to change her behaviour, and every morning on her way into work she would ask the Archangels Michael, Gabriel, Chamuel and Raphael to form a protective circle around her so that she would project the energies of strength, courage and love for herself. Her colleagues picked up on this new-found energy almost instantly, and she regained her power in the office, and professional and social situations began to go in her favour.

Bereavement

Grief

Grief is a very strong emotion and is a reaction to loss, either through the ending of a relationship or through bereavement. While grieving, people may lose touch with their reality because of the trauma they are dealing with and find it very difficult adjusting back to normal life. Bitterness and anger may consume the person who is grieving, and this anger may stay within them but become directed externally, either towards people or to life in general. Angels provide comfort and wait patiently until you are ready to accept healing for your grief.

Loss

If you have lost a loved one, you may be feeling shocked and disconnected. Life may no longer seem real, or even worth living at times. The Angels ask that you remember love and cherish the beautiful memories shared between you. Saying goodbye and letting go can be the most difficult thing you face as a result of this loss, as it makes you acknowledge that it really has happened. Knowing that you did your best for the person throughout your togetherness and took the time to tell them at each opportunity that you loved them will help you to come to terms with your loss. Angels will help you to transmute unhappiness, guilt, regret or sorrow into love so that you can begin your healing journey.

Comfort

Angels will comfort you during your lowest points, however you may be so consumed with negative energy that you will not perceive this energy through any of your senses. You may have completely given up on any type of faith and reject any form of help. This is completely understandable, as such overwhelming sadness disconnects your soul from your body, and your mind from your heart. The Angels will give you reassurance that you will cope and that you will return to normal life eventually. They will continuously help you in your grief and stop you from falling apart.

Counselling

Sometimes, nothing anyone can say or do will help. Angels will get you through, day by day, until you are ready to heal the pain and breathe again. The Angels will never give up on you, even if you give up on them. They will wait until you are ready to speak about your pain, either to them or to a trusted counsellor or friend. During times of grief, your connection to the Angels may not be strong enough for you to fully communicate with them, so they will speak to and guide other people into your life who can relay their advice and guidance to you. Angels want you to know that you are not alone and that, at times like these, your relationship with others will deepen as you receive support from them.

Spirit

If you have experienced bereavement, the soul of your loved one has now transcended into a different realm, the spiritual realm. Much like the Angels, the soul does not actually have a physical form. It enters the body at birth to embody love and to have the

Earthly experience. An unhealthy attachment to the soul which has now passed from the body will hold the soul back from progressing along its journey. This may also apply to the ending of a relationship. You will no longer be together in physical form, however the person's soul will always reside in your memory and in your hearts will now be a guiding star above you.

Patience

Angels know that grieving is a natural emotion and they will have complete patience while you see this process through. They will help you to keep the memory of the one you have lost alive in your heart without it being too painful for you. They want you to believe that the love you have shared is timeless and they will give you the energy to move into your future with hope. You will be able to hear or feel their presence by changing your awareness to receive their messages of love.

ANGEL HEALING MEDITATION FOR BEREAVEMENT

ANGEL SECRET:

'After all endings there is a new beginning.'

CROWN CHAKRA

Angel Starlight enters your angelic body through a beautiful white rose just above your physical body. You see a silvery sparkling star in the centre of your crown chakra and connect through it with your soul. It may be looking quite small or broken, through the grief that you have experienced. Your Guardian Angel is now shining the Angel Starlight into your soul to call back all the components and elements of your soul and piece them back together again. This process is called soul retrieval. See that hundreds of tiny silvery sparkles of light are now coming into your soul to make it whole again.

THIRD-EYE CHAKRA

Angel Starlight travels down into the purple rose between your two eyes and into your mind. It begins to clear any blocks on your intuition. Your Guardian Angel takes you to a healing sanctuary. Visualize yourself in a white Heavenly temple where your body, mind, heart and soul will be cleansed of all toxins. Send yourself into a very deep state of relaxation by counting back from seven to one, very slowly. As you relax more and more, you will be able to absorb the healing properties of the Angel Starlight.

THROAT CHAKRA

Angel Starlight travels down into the blue rose in your throat and extends towards your ears. Your Guardian Angel now helps you to communicate about your loss. See and feel the Angel Starlight energy running through into your throat area, removing the dark, dense energy that has built up and created a block in your throat chakra. If you need more energy, call upon Archangel Michael by saying, 'Dear Archangel Michael, please connect with me now and unblock my throat chakra so that I can release my negative emotions. Thank you.'

HEART CHAKRA

Angel Starlight travels down into the green rose within your heart and, as it blossoms, you see that it slowly transforms into a pink rose. Your Guardian Angel asks you to breathe in the energy of love and breathe out the energy of sadness. Repeat this at least ten times, until you feel your heart becoming emotionally and physically stronger. It may feel difficult for you to accept healing into your heart, for many reasons. If negative emotions such as guilt, regret or anger come up, measure the strength of these and watch as they dissolve with the Angel Starlight from ten on the scale to one.

SOLAR PLEXUS CHAKRA

Angel Starlight travels down into the yellow rose within your stomach area, the core of your being. Your Guardian Angel is now shining the Angel Starlight into this area. See that you now have a powerful sun in the centre of your being. The sun's rays are now melting away any stress, anger, guilt and regret relating to your loss. As these emotions melt away, the feeling of acceptance replaces them and starts flowing up towards your heart, up towards your soul, then back down into your solar plexus. Repeat 5–10 times.

SACRAL CHAKRA

Angel Starlight travels down into the orange rose just below your navel and activates your creative abilities. Your Guardian Angel shows you the energetic cord which is attached between you and the person you have lost. See that Angel Starlight is running through this cord and carrying the purest unconditional love between your souls. If it feels right to telepathically communicate with each other, then ask your Guardian Angel for guidance to interpret the messages coming between you. As the soul of your loved one has connected with you and your channel of love has been cleansed, you will feel closer to them, and in time you will feel that, even though they are not with you physically, they are in your heart.

ROOT CHAKRA

Angel Starlight travels down into the red rose at the base of your spine. Look very deeply within this red rose as your Guardian Angel brings your awareness to your physical body. As this is a very intense healing exercise, it is very important that you bring your whole energy back into your body. Visualize and feel your aura contracting closer to your body, your chakras beginning to close down and the golden Angel Starlight washing away all the excess energy around your body.

Success Story

Anne had Angel Healing to help her through her grief at losing her brother. The sudden and unexpected loss had a very distressing effect on all members of the family, and Anne experienced it very profoundly, as she had looked up to her brother as a father figure. Because he lived abroad, she never got the chance to say goodbye. During her meditation, Anne was asked if she was ready to let go of her grief. She found this extremely difficult, as she believed it was the same as letting go of the love she had for her brother. She was told that healing would be available for her when she felt ready. Anne had a few Angel Healing sessions, which gave her comfort and strength. It was a year or so later that she was ready to let go, and her session was incredibly emotional and intense. During her meditation, she was taken to the spiritual realm, to reunite with her brother and communicate with him. There was so much she wished she had told him, and this was an opportunity to release her words and emotions. He told her that he loved her like a daughter, and that she was an Angel on earth and needed to get her life and health back on track, as she had a huge purpose to serve. She sobbed uncontrollably throughout this session and could not make the promise. She admitted that a part of her wanted to be with her brother rather than continuing her life in such misery. At that moment, she was given the choice of giving up on life or coming back into her body as a healed and strong person with loving memories of her brother in her heart. The Angels showed me that there was a column of white light shining upon her; I could see it very clearly. Anne decided that she wanted to continue with her life and accepted the healing. After the session, Anne felt alive again, with a strong purpose of living – especially as her brother showed her that the gift of a grandchild would be coming into her life very soon! After ten or more years of grieving, Anne was able to live her life every day, thanking her brother for watching over her and her family from the spirit world.

Heartbreak

Relationship Ended

If you are heartbroken because a relationship has come to an end with the one you loved, believe that there is a hidden blessing to why it has happened. When you open your heart to another person with love, you begin another journey, and when you have completed the cycle of learning through your relationship, it may be time to move on. As you go through these cycles, your energetic frequencies change and, depending on the dynamics of your relationship, you will either become more negative or more positive. To understand the important role your partner has played in your life, and his or her purpose and gift to you, ask the Angels to bring you clarity. Healing a broken heart takes time and patience. Ask your Guardian Angel to be with you and to communicate with you through writing or direct channelling to explain the reason for your pain, what you could have done better or less of, what the other person was going through emotionally, what they have learned and if the differences between you are irreconcilable. Those whom you love and open your heart to are your greatest teachers. They bring you an opportunity to experience love in all its forms, and no matter what the outcome or ending may be, there is always a hidden blessing.

Betrayal of Trust

Angels know how difficult it is to put trust in others. Due to the negative influence of previous failed relationships you may have experienced or witnessed, your mind may become sceptical, and the heart erects barriers so that it will not be broken again. These barriers around your heart slowly come down as you allow the person in. Angels say that the problem with this is that you start the relationship with expectations, on a deep level of your consciousness, of being betrayed, so unfortunately, what you hold within you at this level will more than likely manifest itself to become your reality. Ask your Guardian Angel to send healing to your previous experiences of being betrayed and to transmute the fear into unconditional love on all levels so that you come to believe only in positive relationships and outcomes. This is your part of the responsibility. How the other person chooses their actions is something that you cannot control, other than to communicate with them effectively to ensure they are being honest about their emotions towards you and your relationship. If you have been betrayed through infidelity, Angel Healing will help you regain your confidence, self-esteem and forgiveness so that you can move forward.

Disappointment

Angels are able to lift you from your disappointment in the person who has broken your heart with their compassion. Although it is your right to feel let down or betrayed and to be angry about that, these negative feelings can lead to more serious issues on other levels of your angelic body. By asking your Guardian Angel for the energy of compassion, you will begin to see things from the other person's perspective and it will also highlight any unreasonable or unhealthy dependencies you may have subconsciously placed upon them. You can only feel disappointment towards someone if you have judged them or their actions. When you live your life without judging others and remain true to your values, you release the possibility of being heartbroken. If you communicate your expectations to the people you love at the start of any relationship, you can work together to respect each other's values. What may be completely acceptable to one person may not be acceptable to you, therefore the feeling of being disappointed in someone is arises from having disrespected their opinions by judging them. Angels help you find compassion for others when you ask them to, and they also help you to become less judgemental. If you choose to dwell on disappointments in the past, believing that the more you love, the more your heart will be broken, you will remain stagnant. However, if you choose to believe that the more you love, the more you will grow, you fearlessly move forward towards happiness.

Dishonesty

Angels are able to help to unfold any dishonesty by raising your intuitive awareness. If you believe that you are being lied to by someone you love, Angels will also help you to approach the subject in a way that will not cause arguments. You may be feeling very heartbroken because you have found out that the person you loved has lied to you. Ask your Guardian Angel to help you get to the real reason for their dishonesty. Most of the time, dishonesty occurs because the other person has been trying to protect the person they love. It is important to understand the real cause of the dishonesty in order to be able to compromise. Once this has been communicated and understood by everyone involved, this will repair any damage caused in trusting each other.

Attachments

Unhealthy attachments to those you love may cause heartbreak. Angels say this is because you give your power, independence and freedom over into the hands of the person you love. Being in a relationship shouldn't mean that you lose these qualities, because that means that you begin to lose your identity. Angels are able to help you identify any unhealthy attachments towards others because you may be subconsciously holding them back from being their true selves. It is mostly because of this that dishonesty occurs, because the person you love may not feel free enough to express themselves and so take the chance of doing it behind your back, hoping that they will not be caught. Ask your Guardian Angel to heal the unhealthy attachments you know you have, even if you have denied this to yourself for a long time. This will set you and the other person free, and you will reduce the chances of being lied to. Then your relationship will have the chance to develop in a very healthy manner. Happiness comes from loving and appreciating others, yet being physically, mentally, emotionally and spiritually independent.

Blame and Responsibility

Angels say that healing begins when you believe that you are responsible for your emotions, your thoughts, your actions and your state of being. Blaming another person for the mistakes that they have made is a complete waste of your precious energy, as there is no resolution or learning that can ever come from blame. Acceptance that whatever has happened is somehow in line with your life plan will stop you from brewing feelings of anger, hate, resentment and all other negative emotions. These can never serve you in a positive way, therefore your Guardian Angel will show you your own responsibility in the situation that has caused you heartbreak. If you have had many past experiences which have left you heartbroken, the trauma stays within your emotional body and will grow into victim energy, in which you start to believe that the world is against you. Angel Healing will remove the layers of these traumatic events and will cleanse your emotional body until you begin to feel in control.

ANGEL HEALING MEDITATION FOR HEARTBREAK

ANGEL SECRET:

'As love cannot be broken, neither can the heart, as it is made of love.'

CROWN CHAKRA

Angel Starlight enters your angelic body through a beautiful white rose just above your physical body. You see a silvery sparkling star in the centre of your crown chakra and connect with your soul. As you connect with your soul, listen to its wisdom about what the purpose of your heartbreak was and what your learning is. Visualize your soul shining brighter as it is now filling your whole body with Angel Starlight so that you can begin your healing journey. Your Guardian Angel will now connect you with the other person's soul.

THIRD-EYE CHAKRA

Angel Starlight travels down into the purple rose between your two eyes and into your mind. It now begins to clear any blocks on your intuition. Your Guardian Angel shows you how the person who has broken your heart is feeling. Use your intuition to see, hear and feel what is going on in their life. Can you tell by their aura if they feel guilty about their actions? If you feel ready to confront them, see yourself walking closer towards them, with your Guardian Angel standing behind you. The Angel Starlight is now being poured into you both from high above, transmuting all the negative emotions between you so that you can continue with the healing journey.

THROAT CHAKRA

Angel Starlight travels down into the blue rose in your throat and extends towards your ears. Your Guardian Angel helps you to communicate all your feelings of hurt to this person. Explain how long you have felt this way, all the wrongdoings on your part and their part. Talk about what you have learned from this situation and what you will not be taking forward into your next relationship. Listen carefully as the soul of the other person communicates things from their perspective, and be ready to accept what they are about to tell you about how you made them feel. Once all communication has finished, visualize the two of you growing into angelic beings and glowing with the golden Angel Starlight flowing between you.

HEART CHAKRA

Angel Starlight travels down into the green rose within your heart and, as it blossoms, you see that it slowly transforms into a pink rose. Your Guardian Angel now surrounds you both in unconditional love and respect for each other as the Angel Starlight now dissolves any hurt feelings, regrets, guilt and all memories of the bad experiences you had, leaving you with only the good memories of love, respect and gratitude for all that you have shared together.

SOLAR PLEXUS CHAKRA

Angel Starlight travels down into the yellow rose within your stomach area, the core of your being. Your Guardian Angel now gives you the courage to walk away from this person and allows you both to go your own separate ways. Ask yourself if this is what you really want to do or whether you want to rekindle your relationship without any resentment towards the person. The Angel Starlight energy is now empowering you to make the choice that is best for you. If you feel you need the energy of forgiveness, ask that your Guardian Angel gives this to you now.

SACRAL CHAKRA

Angel Starlight travels down into the orange rose just below your navel and activates your creative abilities. Your Guardian Angel now takes you on a journey into your future. The Angel Starlight removes the fears you are holding within you about seeing your future and being with another person. As you travel deeper through the orange colours, you become stronger, empowered and determined to change your life for the better. You see yourself moving forward with peace in your heart. There is no bitterness within you, only love for yourself and for your life.

ROOT CHAKRA

Angel Starlight travels down into the red rose at the base of your spine. Look very deep within this red rose as your Guardian Angel sends Angel Starlight energy through your whole body, washing away all traces of heartbreak and giving you a new lease of life. You are ready to move forward with your dignity, and knowing that you deserve to be in a beautiful, trusting relationship. Repeat the affirmation: 'Angel Starlight has now healed my broken heart.'

Success Story

Bea came to Angel Healing in search of healing for heartbreak. She had been suffering from mild heart problems whereby she experienced irregular heartbeats, especially when she was upset or stressed. During her meditation, her Guardian Angel revealed Bea's heart to be in a weakened condition and asked Bea to feel that all the heartbreak over the years was being pulled out of her. As Bea released these emotions, she recognized that the healing energy was slowly breaking down the protective barriers around her heart. Archangel Chamuel and the love Angels began filling her with unconditional love and compassion. Bea saw that her physical heart was becoming stronger in every way as a beautiful pink light of love flowed through each artery and ran through her bloodstream, cleansing her body, mind, heart and soul and purifying every single cell in her body. She felt consumed with love and could no longer feel any negativity towards herself, others or her life. Within days of her session, Bea reported that she was a lot happier within herself and was hopeful that she could love again without the fear of being hurt by others. Suddenly, she had become very popular and was attracting new friends and wonderful opportunities into her life.

Forgiveness

Peace

Every moment that has just passed is your past. When negative emotions from the past are stored within you and carried into your present moment, you are creating a negative future which will be in your next moment. Whatever has caused upheaval in your life needs to be acknowledged and given to your Guardian Angel to transmute back into love. Forgiveness actually means 'for giving'. The longer you hang on to what is not serving you, the more it will consume you. Your peace is precious and sacred, and only you should have control of it.

Injustice

Angels ask you to open your heart and understand the reasons for injustices. Some good will come from bad situations when you understand what learning can be derived from what has happened. Compassion will give you the strength to forgive. Negative cords are created when there is conflict, separation or emotional distress between people, and where injustices have occurred. Even if you have physically moved on from someone who may have caused any of these in your past, the cords will remain attached between you spiritually, therefore you may mentally or emotionally remember what you lived through with that person. Through Angel Healing you can ask that these invisible negative cords between you are cut. This way, you are energetically cutting your ties in order to release and surrender the situation.

Regrets

If you have been taken advantage of in a relationship, you may be regretting opening your heart to that person, and this feeling will have a negative impact on your ability to love again. Forgiveness comes from understanding and accepting the situation you are faced with. It is not condoning the other person's actions or accepting that what they have done is all right. When you are ready and willing to move forward emotionally, mentally and physically, you will be motivated to forgive and forget. Although it may seem that those who forgive are weak, it actually takes a very strong person to be able to forgive. Forgiveness is a way of finding peace and freedom. Being mentally trapped in resentment or hatred will keep you in a negative place emotionally, and your emotions will change to anger. These emotions will find a way to be expressed one way or another, either by you punishing yourself or punishing others.

Review

To understand how and why a negative situation has occurred, look at the responsibilities of all those involved. If you were genuinely mistreated through no fault or responsibility of your own, try to understand the other person's position and behaviour. To accept the situation, try to see the positive that has arisen from it. You may feel that there is absolutely no positive thing that has come out of it and that you will never forgive the other person for hurting, betraying or bullying you. By changing your perspective, you will find the lesson that your soul has learned and how it can now grow from it. Before you can understand the actions of others, you need to understand your own actions and how you attracted the particular situation into your reality. Holding grudges will stop you from moving forward and will keep you energetically trapped in bitterness. Angels look at situations through the eyes of unconditional love at all times. If you are able to practise this, no matter how big or small the situations you are faced with throughout your life, you will learn to be at peace at all times.

Purpose

Each relationship is as important as the next one, because you may not be able to attract the next one if you don't grow from the previous one! Challenges and difficulties in relationships act as catalysts to move you towards your most compatible partner. If you had no partner to hold the mirror up to you so that you can look within, you would never know what is acceptable or not. When the purpose of each relationship has been achieved, take from it the experience and the love, not the negativity, as this holds you in the past. Forgiveness sets you free. Angel Healing will help you to confront the bitter emotions the experience has left with you and then remove them. It is not necessary for you to tell the people you are forgiving, just releasing the emotions attached to them will cut the negative emotions between you and you will find that you no longer even remember them.

ANGEL HEALING MEDITATION FOR FORGIVENESS

ANGEL SECRET:

'There is no need to forgive when you believe love is for giving.'

CROWN CHAKRA

Angel Starlight enters your angelic body through a beautiful white rose just above your physical body. You see a silvery sparkling star in the centre of your crown chakra and connect with your soul. Your Guardian Angel takes away your pain and hurt so that you can start the forgiveness process. See that your soul is shining more brightly as any sign of sadness in your heart, mind and body now melts away with the light of your soul. Spend a few moments watching your soul shine its bright light and qualities to all areas of your angelic body.

THIRD-EYE CHAKRA

Angel Starlight travels down into the purple rose between your two eyes and into your mind. It begins to clear any blocks on your intuition. Your Guardian Angel shows you a review of your situation from start to finish. Look into your relationship with the person involved and, as you picture them, you see through their rough exterior and connect with their heart. In your mind's eye, you see all the arguments and negativity being washed away with a waterfall of golden Angel Starlight energy. This energy washes over all those involved and the places that you have been together, such as the home, workplace, car, etc.

THROAT CHAKRA

Angel Starlight travels down into the blue rose in your throat and extends towards your ears. Your Guardian Angel helps you to start feeling much more relaxed and positive, and you are now ready to forgive and set yourself free energetically. Hear yourself telling the person that you are ready to forgive them, but this does not mean that you are condoning their actions. Ask them if they have learned from their mistakes and listen to what they have to say.

HEART CHAKRA

Angel Starlight travels down into the green rose within your heart and, as it blossoms, you see that it slowly transforms into a pink rose. Your Guardian Angel now helps you to find the unconditional love with your heart. Visualize that all the negative cords extending from your heart to those who have hurt you in the past are being cut. Now feel that a large, dark cord is being pulled from your heart chakra and see that it is pulled from the heart chakra of the person who you are forgiving as well. The golden Angel Starlight is now filling both your hearts with love.

SOLAR PLEXUS CHAKRA

Angel Starlight travels down into the yellow rose within your stomach area, the core of your being. Your Guardian Angel gives you the feeling of freedom to move on with your life. Know that you have both been each other's teachers throughout your relationship and that you are actually very grateful for their teachings. As you travel deeper into your solar plexus area, look for any patterns of power struggles, pride or ego you have with regard to forgiveness. Watch these melt away and become transmuted into your natural power.

SACRAL CHAKRA

Angel Starlight travels down into the orange rose just below your navel and activates your creative abilities. Your Guardian Angel now reconnects you to your dignity, knowing and believing that you are true to yourself. The Angel Starlight now shines upon this area, enhancing your self-respect and giving you the feeling of respecting others. You now look into your future relationships and see that you have the wisdom never to allow the same situation to happen again and therefore forgiveness will never again be required.

ROOT CHAKRA

Angel Starlight travels down into the red rose at the base of your spine. As the Angel Starlight flows through this area, you go on a journey of self-forgiveness. Your Guardian Angel will now be helping you to be completely truthful and honest about all the guilt and regrets you are holding within yourself from your earliest memory. As they individually come into your mind, hand them over to your Guardian Angel for transmuting into peace, which returns back to you, and to all the people involved in those situations. Repeat the affirmation: 'Angel Starlight is now helping me to forgive.'

Success Story

John had Angel Healing because he was unable to forgive his father, who had abandoned him and his mother when he was very young, leaving them to struggle both financially and emotionally when he was growing up. During his reading, the Angels showed me that he was bitter towards his father and that the resentment within him was causing him to be depressed. As John grew older, he became the man of the house and felt responsible for his mother's happiness, so he would feel guilty if he wasn't always there for her. This had an adverse effect on his personal relationships, and because his sense of abandonment was deeply embedded within his subconscious mind, this pattern persisted throughout his adult life. He had been cheated on and abandoned by his wife, as well as having been made redundant from his job, and he was often neglected by friends and colleagues. In the course of his meditation, the Angels sent healing all the way back to his past, and with the help of Archangel Michael's energy, he was able to cut the negative cords attaching him to the bitterness he felt towards his father. He realized that he was attracting situations which confirmed his negative belief that he deserved to be neglected and abandoned. After his session, he became consciously aware of the negative outlook he had on relationships, and that it was influenced by the failure of his parents' marriage. John went on to attract a secure and happy relationship, and adopted his partner's child, who had been abandoned by her previous partner, thus completing the healing circle.

Finding Love and Romance

Relating

Angels say that the mastery of relating to another person comes when you have mastered relating to yourself. Going through a journey of self-discovery will allow you to embrace your own good qualities while accepting your negative traits. You have free will to change any of these qualities if you cannot accept them. Hiding these negative traits will mean that you may not ever fully love yourself. Trying to make yourself more attractive by denying parts of yourself may backfire in the long term, as you are not being true to yourself or to the other person.

Perfection

Your angelic self is pure and has the natural beauty of innocence. Angel Healing removes all the layers of insecurities and doubts about your natural perfection, and the Angels ignite your inner light so that it can shine through your eyes, smile and heart. Trying to create the perfect external world with material belongings will lead only to short-term excitement and happiness. Once the excitement is over, you are still left with the emptiness within. Perfection of your inner world will shine through into the external world, and create perfection in each moment. With regard to finding the perfect person in a relationship, unfortunately this may be a misconception, as each person has a different definition of the word 'perfect', what values and belief systems this represents. Rather than looking for your ideal 'perfect' relationship, learning to love others perfectly will give lasting results in all relationships.

Inspiration

Angels say that competition between people and especially couples is healthy only if the energy that comes from this competition is the positive aspect of inspiration rather than the negative aspect of jealousy. It is much healthier to be with someone who inspires you and possesses the qualities you want to develop within yourself. This will keep you interested in each other, and you will both be developing each other's weaknesses until you become a perfectly compatible couple. Your Guardian Angel can help you to look within your heart to find the weaknesses your potential partner could help you to develop. Perfect couples will perfectly balance each other out, in that one's strengths are the other's weaknesses. The goal of achieving the perfect relationship is attainable when there is mutual respect and patience as you grow in different directions yet become and remain compatible on all emotional, mental, physical and spiritual levels.

Expectation

What do you really want from a relationship? It is important for you to know this and to have reasonable expectations of it and of the other person, as it will lead to disappointments if your expectations are not fulfilled. Common reasonable expectations such as decency, fidelity, respect and trust aside, think about what your expectations and intentions are. Be true to yourself and to the other person involved about your top priorities and what you are prepared to tolerate. Each person has a different list of values, so what is high priority to them may not be for you. This is why communication is the most important factor in making relationships work and last. Angels will guide you to attract the most compatible partner for you at that moment in your life. As you are continuously changing and growing through life experiences, your personality also changes, so a certain type you used to be attracted to may no longer be attractive to you at later stages in your life.

Romance

The Angels want to help you to find a beautiful loving relationship where you can experience romance, but they ask that you work to become romantic towards yourself first so that you know what the feeling is like. This means completely indulging in things that make you happy, things that make you feel wonderful and special. Ask your Guardian Angel to guide you to find perfect spa days, to buy beautiful flowers and experience the beauty of nature. As you accept the Angel Starlight into your heart, it will flow into your relationship and all other areas of your life. It will magically reinforce the energy of romance back into your relationship to rekindle the passion. Where there is no passion, there is no excitement therefore there is no enthusiasm to move towards fulfilment.

Fulfilment

Angels say that fulfilment comes from believing that you are living your life to the fullest, exploring, experiencing and expressing as much love as possible. The Angels can help you to find the missing link to your fulfilment so that you can enjoy your relationship and your life in the best way. Fulfilment means feeling full of energy on all levels of your being; that is, physically, mentally, emotionally and spiritually. It is not reasonable to expect your partner to fulfil you on all these levels. Angels will guide you to do as much as you can to bring the spark back into your relationship, but they say that individuals should take responsibility for their contentment. If you have grown apart from your partner and you are finding it difficult to be compatible, this could be why you feel unfulfilled. Angel Healing can give you the courage to face the truth that this relationship is not what you want and will help your transition away from it to be much smoother. Angels will give you comfort and reassurance that you are on the right path once you've made your decision.

ANGEL HEALING MEDITATION FOR FINDING LOVE AND ROMANCE

ANGEL SECRET:

'Love is the planted seed, romance is the water and you are the flower.'

CROWN CHAKRA

Angel Starlight enters your angelic body through a beautiful white rose just above your physical body. You see a silvery sparkling star in the centre of your crown chakra and connect with your soul. Your Guardian Angel now cleanses all levels of your angelic body with the energy of purity. Visualize that your soul is renewed, purified and ready to attract love and romance into your life.

THIRD-EYE CHAKRA

Angel Starlight travels down into the purple rose between your two eyes and into your mind. It now begins to clear any blocks on your intuition. Your Guardian Angel shows you how to love, nurture and cherish yourself with romance before you can expect anyone else to do it for you. Visualize a golden piece of paper with a few main priorities that you are expecting from a special relationship written on it. The Angel Starlight now shines upon this golden piece of paper and you see that it shrinks into a small star which is then placed into your soul.

THROAT CHAKRA

Angel Starlight travels down into the blue rose in your throat and extends towards your ears. Your Guardian Angel guides you down a beautiful golden path. Up above in the blue sky, a beautiful sparkling star descends towards you. As it gets closer to you, it takes a human form. You feel so happy to meet this soul and feel that your heart is expanding with so much love. As your souls communicate in the language of love, the feeling of fun, laughter and joy expands throughout your whole body. You travel back along the path with this other soul and know that your Guardian Angel is behind you both, guiding you on your way.

HEART CHAKRA

Angel Starlight travels down into the green rose within your heart and, as it blossoms, you see that it slowly transforms into a pink rose. Your Guardian Angel connects you with the energy of patience. You feel that they also plant a seed into the core of your heart chakra and, as you water it, it fully blossoms into true love. Your partner's soul now leaves an impression in your heart so, when you finally meet in person, your hearts will recognize each other's souls.

SOLAR PLEXUS CHAKRA

Angel Starlight travels down into the yellow rose within your stomach area, the core of your being. Your Guardian Angel directs the Angel Starlight into each cell of your body, and gives you the reassurance that you are loved by many people for the person that you are. You are now ready to make plans to improve upon your weaknesses, preparing to start your new journey with your new partner.

SACRAL CHAKRA

Angel Starlight travels down into the orange rose just below your navel and activates your creative abilities. Your Guardian Angel now takes you back to your happiest ever memory. As you remember this moment in your life, whether it was your most romantic moment or a very happy occasion, you bring that energy back into your body, mind and heart. This changes the energetic vibes that you will be projecting out into the world therefore you will attract even more happy and special moments.

ROOT CHAKRA

Angel Starlight travels down into the red rose at the base of your spine. As you travel through this chakra, bring your awareness to your physical body. The Angel Starlight is now shining into every cell of your body giving you the feelings of beauty and melting away any negative feelings which may be causing you some insecurity about your attractiveness. Visualize yourself looking, feeling and being very comfortable in your own skin. You are now ready and waiting for your compatible partner to physically show up in your life. Repeat the affirmation: 'Angel Starlight is filling me with love and romance.'

Success Story

After waiting for love to appear in my life in the form of a special relationship, over the years of my spiritual development and Angel Healing, I was gradually beginning to find love for myself, my life and for everyone. The love I felt was being projected from my inner world to my external world. My awakening to the purest form of unconditional love came through a chance meeting with someone who came briefly into my life when I was praying to my Angels for a relationship. Although this meeting never developed into a relationship, it awakened a spark deep within my heart. Together, we shared a few special moments which were platonic yet ecstatic on all levels. I began spreading the energy of divine love in every step I took in my life. I wanted to hang on to my connection to this person, but my Angels told me it was time to say goodbye; he had served his purpose. I feel lucky to have experienced such divine love energy, and it inspired me to spread my Angel wings and fly! Rather than continuing to look for love, from that experience onwards, I have naturally attracted the most loving, kind, angelic people into my life, and through them I continue to experience unconditional love.

Practical Exercises with Archangel Chamuel
(Channelling Pink Unconditional Love for Healing the Heart)

Loneliness

Reminiscing on the past keeps you in the past. Before you can move forward and heal your loneliness, think about what you may think were the best days of your life for one last time by holding a special ceremony of closure, so that you can let go of the past and move forward. You may even want to set the scene with candles and wine, and have one last chance to speak to the person as though they are with you in the room. If you can follow this through and say goodbye once and for all, you will be free by having closure. Ask my group of love Angels to join you during your ceremony and to take away any negative memories you have within or around you. For the last time, relive the loving memories in your mind and feel the emotions welling up in your heart. When you are emotionally free from the past, you will be able to fill the space of loneliness with new love. No more confusion and no more loneliness, just cherishing all the nice moments shared. Store away all belongings reminding you of the person in a memory box and place a lid over the treasures in your heart.

Rejection

Allow me to expand your heart and fill it with love. Hold your palms out in front of you as a pink ball of unconditional love is placed within them. In a few moments, place the energetic ball into your heart chakra and know that this is a gift to you from the angelic realm. You may be feeling as though the love you expressed for another being has been rejected, neglected or unappreciated. My love Angels ask you to accept our gift of love as reciprocation for the love you have had rejected. Follow the guidance of the love Angels as they whisper directions that will lead you towards meeting a lovely person who will accept and reciprocate your love. Ask the love Angels to help you to accept yourself and to accept that it's time to move forward. Say the following prayer every day: 'Dear Archangel Chamuel and the love Angels, please fill my heart with unconditional love towards myself, others and for my life. Thank you!'

Bullying

If you find yourself constantly running away from bullying, it's time to look deep within to find your stability, security and strength. Ask yourself the following questions. Where are the energies of stability, security and strength lacking in your life? It will probably be these areas of your life where the bullying is taking place. Then ask yourself, where is stability, security and strength lacking within you? Ask the love Angels to discontinue the bullying by helping you to develop theses three 'S's in your life and within you, on physical, mental, emotional and spiritual levels. Each time you feel like a victim, take this review and work on enhancing these qualities. As you become more stable, secure and strong, bullying comes to an end. Reclaim your power using love. Direct unconditional love towards the bully to open their heart to compassion and love.

Bereavement

Between endings and beginnings, there is a small, empty space of time called 'transition'. Throughout the life of the soul, you will experience many transitions which may seem painful, however, they are necessary for your personal growth, development and evolution. The love Angels wish to bestow their unconditional love to heal the loss you are experiencing on a physical level and to continue the loving memory on the mental, emotional and spiritual levels. To ease your pain, hold a ceremony to celebrate the memory of the person you have lost. This will help you to connect with them beyond the physical realms and in a much deeper, personal way. You will feel, believe and understand that they are in a happy place and that they wish for you also to be happy. This will assist you in coming to terms with change.

Heartbreak

If you feel heartbroken by actions inflicted upon you, give yourself some time to allow the negative thoughts to linger in your mind and the negative emotions to linger in your heart. This gives you a sense that you are rationalizing things and planning an act of revenge as a reaction. This is human nature, but based only on your lower consciousness of the ego. In fact, you will realize that by energizing these negative thoughts and emotions, you are entering a battle zone and setting yourself up for more disappointment. Even if you achieve your revenge, this will only create a short-term victory and, on a deeper level, you may feel guilty or regretful for reacting in a way that doesn't suit your character. When you are ready to heal, thank the person, either mentally or verbally, for coming into your life, teaching you a lesson and showing you something about yourself that you didn't realize before. Thank them for testing your patience and your ability to have unconditional love and compassion for all. Say the following: 'With much love and gratitude, I thank you for everything, and I ask you to leave my body, mind, heart and soul. I now release you to the light.'

Forgiveness

The process of forgiving another person can only begin when you forgive yourself first. Start off by counting the many situations you may need to forgive yourself for, from your earliest memory, then continue, saying, 'I now forgive myself for the roles and responsibilities I had in this situation, with this person.' Every time you forgive yourself for something, the love Angels reward you with many gifts of love, freedom, compassion, peace, joy, happiness, and so on. Hold out your arms to receive and place each one of these gifts in your heart as you forgive yourself. Once you have completely forgiven yourself, close your eyes and see the person you need to forgive standing in front of you. With the gifts given to you by the love Angels, you now possess all the qualities you need to forgive the person. As a gift back to the Angels, spread these beautiful qualities and angelic love to as many people in the world as possible at every opportunity. Unconditional love means giving love with no conditions placed upon receiving love back.

Finding Love and Romance

Love letters are a very effective way of releasing your loving emotions, as well as being very romantic. Write a love letter to your current, or future, partner, explaining how much you love them in every way possible. Express the affection you yearn to show them and that you look forward to sharing a very happy life together. Let the contents of this letter be channelled through the depth of your *heart. Do not hold back on anything. Feel liberated as you release your desires for love and romance to fill your life. Store this letter in a special place and ask the love Angels to bring everything you have written about into your life, including the actual person this letter will belong to, if you are currently single. Charge your rose quartz crystal by running it under cold water for a few minutes and then holding it in your palms as the love Angels direct a flow of pink unconditional love into your hands and the stone. During the night, place this rose quartz crystal on your love letter, and during the day, carry your crystal around with you until love and romance present themselves in a magical way.*

PART VIII:

ANGEL HEALING
FOR THE SOUL

This section will cover the main spiritual challenges that people face throughout their lives, especially with regard to understanding the soul's purpose and connections to the body, mind and heart. There will be a short description of each spiritual factor and how it can be applied in everyday life situations. The advice has been directly channelled from the Angels, providing a completely different perspective on the situation. After each section, there is an Angel Healing meditation which will begin to release blocks on an energetic level. The practical exercises provide ideas of action to be taken, and affirmations for the mind to enhance your healing as they change your thought patterns into positivity.

Your soul is also known as the angelic self. When the soul comes into the human body, it attaches to your crown chakra as a sparkling star and is an intermediary between the Creator and your body, mind and heart. The soul has an expansive consciousness which is connected to all that is. This consciousness can be directed into any realm within the universe. There is a silver cord that attaches the soul to the human body until it is time for it to permanently leave the body. During out-of-body experiences, meditations or sleep, this cord will keep your soul attached to your body. The soul enters your body at birth and continues its journey when it passes from the body. The term 'soul searching' means looking for a higher meaning to life. When the soul feels trapped in an unfulfilling relationship, career or generally, it causes the feeling of depression emotionally, stress mentally and very low energy levels on a physical level. These symptoms will push you towards either breaking free or breaking point, and this is usually the beginning of soul awakening – understanding that you are more than a body, mind and heart. Once you acknowledge your soul, you begin to recognize purity and innocence within others, for example, in a soul mate. The term 'soul consciousness' means broadening the narrow vision of life you have consciously and tapping into and using the creative, ancient wisdom and intelligence of your soul to change your life experience for the better. When you are soul conscious you believe in all possibilities and have a clear direction and knowledge of your life purpose. You connect with others on a soul level, seeing past their tough exterior and fear-based ego. The purpose of your soul is to evolve through life experiences. Angels can help you to awaken and connect to your soul so that you can start experiencing life from a higher spiritual perspective. This will give you a sense of purpose in living and will rescue you if you often feel like a lost soul who doesn't belong on Earth.

A soul mate is a friend from home who will awaken the purity of love within you once you find them. You may meet and love many soul mates, so remember to delight in their Heavenly gift to you and hold no resentments if the outcome of the relationship is not what you expect. Know that once the mission is complete, they may walk out and allow another soul mate to walk into your life. Each person has a soul family, and members of this soul family are called soul mates. They come into each other's lives to help with clearing spiritual blocks and karmic debts and to help each other learn. All relationships require work and patience to see the journey through. The ending doesn't matter as, on a spiritual level, there is an energetic cord between you which can never be broken. This cord keeps all soul family members connected until they reunite in another realm or in another lifetime. Soul mates bring each other a very beautiful gift of growth through experiencing such intense soul love. Even if, on the surface, it seems that you have been hurt, disappointed or betrayed, understanding the purpose of your journey together is the most important factor to take away from the experience.

As well as having soul mates, each person also has a twin soul, which has either incarnated on the Earth realm or is guiding you from the spiritual realm. Your relationship with your twin soul is different from that with a soul mate. Soul mates are all part of the same family, but with twin souls, you are one soul, which has been divided into a feminine aspect and a masculine aspect. Each part has experienced many incarnations in both feminine and masculine embodiments in order to become complete again. The existence of your twin soul is what lies beneath the deep feeling of searching for your missing components and your 'other half' throughout life. On a soul level, this search is actually for your twin soul, and this cannot be understood by the conscious mind.

Many lifetimes may have been spent apart from your twin soul, however in some incarnations they may have very strong bonds with you, forming a pairing such as husband/ wife, mother/ son, brother/ sister, etc.

Twin souls usually share similar life journeys and special missions to fulfil. As they are connected on a soul level and share the same energetic blueprints, they will more than likely mirror each other's lives if they are on Earth at the same time. This mirroring occurs on all levels: physically, mentally, emotionally and spiritually. Even if each twin soul is in a different place in the world, each will pick up on the other's emotions and either lift them up or weigh them down with negativity.

The twin soul reunion has a very special purpose of igniting the divine passion within each other's hearts. By coming together, even for a short amount of time, the long-term effects are incredible and very enlightening, especially if you are called to do healing work or to serve humanity on a very large scale.

Awaken Your Soul

Soul Journey

The journey of the soul is eternal. Its home is within the spiritual realm, where it exists in a state of bliss, love and harmony, interacting with many other souls and especially with the members of its soul group or family. Each soul is a particle of the same source or creation and holds infinite intelligence and wisdom. In order for the soul to experience anything other than its natural state of purity, it will go on a journey to incarnate into a realm other than its home. There is a Guardian Angel assigned to each soul who has a responsibility to see the soul through its entire journey, through lives on Earth, in spirit and in between lives. Each soul has a different amount of lives on Earth, and during each one it will incur karmic repercussions for the actions it decided to undertake. Angel Healing helps you to remember, understand and heal any accumulated karma from past lives, in accordance with the law of cause and effect.

Soul's Purpose

The purpose of each soul is to learn, develop and evolve throughout its journey. Each soul is originally created in the purest form of light, like the creator of all that is or universal source energy. As the soul embarks on its journey into different realms and during different eras, its purity becomes diminished. One of the biggest reasons for Angels intervening in our lives on Earth today is to help each soul reawaken to its pure state and consequently end the suffering it is enduring in human form. Many wise souls are reincarnating on Earth at this time as spiritual teachers, healers or counsellors, and they are aware of the angelic presence and energies available to humanity as help. They are aware of their soul's purpose and, with the Angels' guidance, you can learn what your own purpose is. Angel Healing will assist you in awakening your soul consciousness and help you to start listening to your soul and to your Guardian Angels, and to understand that there really is more to life.

Soul Searching

Your soul is your angelic self. It has patiently waited to be acknowledged by your heart, mind and body. After many years of searching for love, you may now realize that actually you have been soul searching. Many people go through life feeling unappreciated, unacknowledged or unloved and therefore become conditioned to believe that they are not worthy. Before you can awaken the Angel within you, you go through hardships and challenges which will eventually push you towards a soul awakening, through soul searching and on a self-healing journey. Your Guardian Angel is with you each step of the way, however Guardian Angels are more proactive during transitional phases in your life. When you invoke them to play a role in your self-healing, your life will transform enormously as you begin to understand that there is more to life than what you have experienced up until that point.

Soul Mission

Your soul waits in the spiritual realm for an opportunity to come to Earth and fulfil a special mission. Unfortunately, this mission is forgotten when the soul enters the human body, and you may spend a whole lifetime trying to understand why you are actually here. As your life changes, your Guardian Angel guides you to meet certain people who will help to put you on the right path so that, eventually, you will find what you are here to do. For example, you may be guided to develop certain skills by working in a certain industry. That industry may not itself be a part of your mission, but as your Guardian Angel knows everything about you and your life, they know these skills will be useful to you and will guide you to do what is necessary for your future. When you achieve each step, you are slowly getting closer to finding the right path. By asking yourself what your greatest passion in life is and thinking about when you feel most rewarded, you will find the answer to what your soul mission is. One of the major activities in your life is your career or work, therefore you will be most fulfilled when you are carrying out your mission through this activity.

ANGEL HEALING MEDITATION TO AWAKEN YOUR SOUL

ANGEL SECRET

'To awaken the sleeping soul, it has to remember itself and achieve its goal.'

CROWN CHAKRA

Angel Starlight enters your angelic body through a beautiful white rose just above your physical body. You see a silvery

sparkling star in the centre of your crown chakra and connect with your soul. Your Guardian Angel is now ready to fully awaken your soul to its highest potential to guide you in the best way. As you focus on your soul, it becomes much brighter and starts growing larger, until it is as large as your physical body. Spend a few moments as your soul blends with the rest of your angelic body.

THIRD-EYE CHAKRA

Angel Starlight travels down into the purple rose between your two eyes and into your mind. It now begins to clear any blocks on your intuition so that you can clearly see the wisdom, beauty, love and brightness of your soul. Your Guardian Angel sends a stream of golden Angel Starlight energy filled with many beautiful, colourful stars coming from above into your whole aura and all your chakras. This energy contains all the memories of your soul's journey, throughout all past lives, your lifetime and even future life times.

THROAT CHAKRA

Angel Starlight travels down into the blue rose in your throat and extends towards your ears. Your Guardian Angel now helps you to expand your throat chakra so that you can channel your soul's wisdom by speaking out loud. You will receive a message regarding your soul awakening, in either a few words or in long sentences. The more you relax, the more you can become one with your highly intelligent soul. Ask your Guardian Angel to help you relax your mind and open your throat chakra even more as you receive the energy of trust. When you feel ready, begin to speak by saying, 'My soul tells me ...' and continue by allowing the words to come out naturally without you thinking about them.

HEART CHAKRA

Angel Starlight travels down into the green rose within your heart and, as it blossoms, you see that it slowly transforms into a pink rose. Your Guardian Angel reunites your soul with your heart. This is a sacred union which will open your heart to unconditional love from this moment and will bring overwhelming happiness into your life.

SOLAR PLEXUS CHAKRA

Angel Starlight travels down into the yellow rose within your stomach area, the core of your being. Your Guardian Angel gives you the feeling of so much gratitude and appreciation for everything and everyone who has played a role in your life to lead you to this special moment. You now understand the reason for any conflicts or difficult situations you have experienced in the past, which were all necessary for your soul awakening. Express your gratitude for every single blessing in your life, starting by saying, 'I am very grateful for my health, I am very grateful for my family and I am very grateful for my happiness.' Continue stating what you are very grateful for, from the smallest thing to the most important thing in your life.

SACRAL CHAKRA

Angel Starlight travels down into the orange rose just below your navel and activates your creative abilities. Your Guardian Angel is now awakening your soul's creative energy so that very soon you will remember your soul's purpose and follow the right path to fulfil this special purpose. Visualize yourself as a beautiful golden Angel with energetic wings rising up out of your body and standing in front of your physical body. Take a few moments to connect your angelic self with your mind and heart before you see it coming back into your body.

ROOT CHAKRA

Angel Starlight travels down into the red rose at the base of your spine. Your Guardian Angel will now show how far you have progressed and grown into a spiritual being and how your life is about to be transformed with the guidance of your soul, the Angel within you. From this moment, negativity will appear only as an illusion to you, as you only believe in love. You now have all the wisdom within you to create your new life.

Success Story

Jennifer came for Angel Healing to help see her through a major life transition. She was feeling very anxious and insecure, as many things in her life had changed suddenly and, as a result, she had the opportunity to review her life and re-create it in a way that would be in line with her truth. During her meditation, Archangel Gabriel connected with her and performed a purifying healing ritual so that Jennifer could free herself of logical restraints and learn to believe that she had to let go of the old to allow in the new. Jennifer believed she was too old to embrace new beginnings, especially regarding her love and work lives. As layer upon layer of embedded patterns left Jennifer's energetic body, she felt much much lighter physically, and she could eventually see a sparkling star within her mind which represented her soul. Immediately, she realized that, for many years, she had been putting up a front and pretending to be the person others wanted her to be. She had already begun to see changes in her friends and social circle, as she was no longer attracted to certain people's energies, actions and behaviour. This made her feel guilty and she cut herself off from these people, which added to her feelings of isolation and confusion. The Angels reassured her that she was going through an awakening to higher realms and therefore no longer recognized herself or her old interests but that she would adjust to her new energies very soon. Shortly after her session, Jennifer called to say that, after a period of soul-searching and isolation, she had decided to go travelling around the world, which had always been her dream. Up until then, she had never had the confidence to follow it through.

Intuition

Senses

Angels say that many people are beginning to accept that they have a sixth sense, however they feel quite fearful about embracing it. Fear of the unknown creates a block in expanding your mind and places barriers around your heart and soul, stopping you from finding the answers that will lead to your happiness and success. There are many 'psychic senses' that you can become aware of which you probably use every single day and take for granted. As well as having your five senses that you are aware of, you also have hidden senses that your soul perceives.

Clairvoyance

Angels can help you to develop your skill of clearly seeing different forms of energy with your mind's eye, in addition to all that you see in a physical form. Creative visualization exercises during meditation are a very beneficial way of expanding your clairvoyance skills. Time does not exist on a soul level; the past, present and future are held in different dimensions which can be looked into with your mind's eye. This is how psychic readings are performed, by changing your focus into a different space. Angels will guide you to practise using your clairvoyance to enable you to see into your day ahead and to pick up on any problems that can be avoided. It is important to use your clairvoyance when you are in a positive frame of mind and feel emotionally balanced. You are in control of when you want to use your clairvoyant skills and are able to open and close your third-eye chakra as you wish.

Clairaudience

Angels are always speaking to you telepathically, especially when you have asked for their guidance and assistance with a particular situation. The challenge is in identifying your own inner talk from that of your Angels. The difference between the two is that your Angels will always speak positively, as they encourage you to move forward with the confidence that there are many possible ways to overcome a situation, whereas your ego mind will want to keep you in a negative place, energizing thoughts in a dramatic way, as though there is no solution to aid you in achieving your goal. The ego mind is designed to hang on to challenges, conflicts and problems and to look for solutions using logic. Take control of your mind's chatter by choosing to hear only the positive, and you'll be able to connect with and listen to your Angels. You will be able to fine-tune the guidance coming from your Angels like you tune a radio station! If it is too loud or too quiet, ask your Angels to meet you in the middle, where it is most comfortable for you. Remember that you are in control of when you want to listen to guidance and when you want to follow your own mind. The Angels will not be offended if you do not take their advice, as they know that you need to learn from your choices, even if there are repercussions involved. Because they love you uncon-ditionally, they will be there to comfort you when things don't go your way.

Clairsentience

You have an angelic body which vibrates at a certain energetic frequency, depending on your physical, mental, emotional and spiritual well-being. Even though you cannot see these waves of energy, they exist and interact with the world you live in, and with other people's angelic bodies. When you meet someone new and either warm to them quite quickly or have a bad feeling about them, you are picking up on their vibes, because you do not, logically, know anything about them. This is a psychic sense known to many people as their gut instinct. The clairsentience skill is held within the solar plexus chakra, and the Angels can help you to enhance this psychic skill by removing all the negative emotions held within this area which not only block your intuition but also result in stress and illness of the stomach or digestive system.

Trust

The most important thing to do when developing your intuition is to trust what you see, hear and feel. This removes the doubt within your mind and shifts your awareness to becoming more soul conscious. Doubt comes from fear of the unknown, which is controlled by your logical mind. Meditation is a tool which enables you to tune into your intuitive senses with the help of your Angels. In time and with practice, you will realize which is your strongest intuitive sense and can then develop that skill until it becomes one of your natural senses. When you practise sharing your intuitive perceptions with others in a sensible way, you may receive validation from their feedback, and this will boost your confidence even more, which leads to trusting and believing in yourself.

ANGEL HEALING MEDITATION FOR INTUITION

ANGEL SECRET:

'Intuition develops by listening to the tuition from within.'

CROWN CHAKRA

Angel Starlight enters your angelic body through a beautiful white rose just above your physical body. You see a silvery sparkling star in the centre of your crown chakra and connect with your soul. Visualize your soul expanding to become as large as your physical body. Become one with your soul now and see that, within a few moments, a golden Angel with energetic wings will emerge from your physical body.

THIRD-EYE CHAKRA

Angel Starlight travels down into the purple rose between your two eyes and into your mind. It now begins to clear your intuition blocks so that you can see the golden Angel within you now coming out of your body. Your angelic self now guides you to activate your third-eye chakra by bringing your right hand to touch your forehead. Visualize a beautiful big purple eye slowly opening in your mind and feel a sense of expansion in between your two physical eyes. You have now fully activated your psychic awareness, and you can use it as often as you wish for your own guidance.

THROAT CHAKRA

Angel Starlight travels down into the blue rose in your throat and extends towards your ears. Your angelic self now comes back into your body and locks in with your throat chakra. Think about an area of your future in which you need some guidance. When you feel ready, activate your throat chakra by beginning to talk from your soul, trusting that this is guidance rather than your imagination. Begin by saying, 'My soul tells me that …' and continue channelling the information coming through you.

HEART CHAKRA

Angel Starlight travels down into the green rose within your heart and, as it blossoms, you see that it slowly transforms into a pink rose. Visualize that your soul is now connected with the purity of your heart. Visualize that the pink unconditional love is now expanding throughout your whole body, filling every part of your being. As you merge with this energy of love, your energetic frequency is rising higher and higher until you feel as if you are floating.

SOLAR PLEXUS CHAKRA

Angel Starlight travels down into the yellow rose within your stomach area, the core of your being. Your natural, inherent clairsentient skills are within this chakra, also known as your gut instinct. Now that the darkness of negative energy has been removed from this chakra, you are able to listen to your psychic feelings more, and to trust them. Tune into a situation or a person and pick up the vibes coming from them. Always remember to protect this chakra, as it is the area though which you absorb others' energies. Practise using your clairsentience to feel the energy of your body and chakras. Ask for Angel Starlight energy to flow into any negative areas and to transmute them into positive light.

SACRAL CHAKRA

Angel Starlight travels down into the orange rose just below your navel and activates your creative abilities. Visualize your angelic self unlocking your highest potential and creativity in relation to your life purpose. Feel the Angel Starlight awakening your angelic art and magical abilities carried forward from past lives and helping you to express them with confidence. Now listen to the language, thought patterns and words used by the people you interact with on a day-to-day basis. Are they blocking your intuition by creating negative thought patterns within your mind? Do they look as if they are having a negative influence on your identity? If so, they may need healing for negative energy, so send them the Angel Starlight.

ROOT CHAKRA

Angel Starlight travels down into the red rose at the base of your spine. Visualize that all the colours of your chakras are merging like a rainbow through your angelic self. You are now able to tap into and use your natural intuition for every decision and action you will take in your future. The more you use your skill for your own healing and guidance, the more it will integrate into your everyday life, and eventually it will become your natural state of being. Repeat the affirmation: 'I am naturally intuitive.'

Success Story

Peter had Angel Healing to heal his fear of using his natural intuitive and psychic skills. In the course of his meditation, while scanning his energetic body, we were both shown that he had a very bright and sensitive aura, which meant that he was almost always using his intuitive senses, even if he wasn't aware he was doing so. The Angels placed a protective shield around his energy so that he wouldn't feel so vulnerable when beginning his journey to develop his intuition. I was told that Peter needed support to be able to trust that his visions and perceptions were not just his imagination, and he booked an ongoing course of development with me. Even though he was aware of his spiritual guides, at first he struggled to open up and allow them to guide him. He needed validation that they actually existed, and we found in his sessions that his Guardian Angel would be the one helping him to achieve this. During one session, Archangel Raphael, the Angel of Intuition, took Peter on a meditation journey into a beautiful healing sanctuary where Peter could let go of all his fears and negative memories from childhood. It appeared that, as a child, he would see and communicate with angelic beings, but when he told his family, they dismissed it. This had ruined his confidence and made him feel inadequate. Once these feelings were released, Peter began to embrace his gift of clairvoyance and, within a few weeks, he was able to channel his spirit guides and Guardian Angel beautifully, as well as being able to read their messages through Angel and Tarot cards.

Cleansing

True Essence

The true essence of your soul is peace, innocence, love and bliss. When your angelic body is constantly cleansed and returns back to purity, you will begin to feel renewed, and even reborn, in every way. This is because, during cleansing, you will literally shed the old energy and replace it with new, vibrant, pure and fresh energy which will go into your whole angelic body. The cleansing will be initially with the Angel Starlight and then with universal life-force energy that exists in every living organism. With a new lease of energy, you will have a new lease of life directing you to take steps in order to achieve your goals and live a very happy life. One thing that you will notice is that the more you cleanse yourself energetically, the more your intuitive and channelling abilities will naturally heighten and your genuine loving self will shine through, attracting more friends and relationships.

Negative Group Consciousness

When you cleanse your body, mind, heart and soul with Angel Healing, you may feel very sensitive to your environment, as your aura and chakras will pick up on everything going on in your world. There are many external factors that may influence your and other people's moods in a harmful way. This is called negative group consciousness: it is completely fear-based and is a form of trying to control others. A few examples are exaggeration of pandemics, financial insecurities, violence and other situations which cause disharmony. Although being aware of what is happening in the world may be beneficial, when listening to or reading only the bad news, it tends to build up within your subconscious mind and subliminally control your life. Angels encourage us to direct healing light, prayer and good, positive thoughts to all these situations, if and when you hear about them. Your positivity does have an influential role to play in resolving these situations and so is more beneficial than joining in and energizing the fear that lies at their root. As you begin to speak positively, word gets around and people will feel more at ease.

Judgement by Others

One of the biggest challenges to maintaining happiness is the judgement of others regarding the way you choose to live your life. This often creates tension in your relationships with them and tension within yourself for not fully being able to follow your heart for fear of disappointing or failing others. Hearing that you are not good enough, worthy, or appreciated for who you are creates a huge block in your confidence. Often, when your ideas, way of life or means of expression do not fit in with those of society, on an energetic level, you will be isolated or even attacked, and this stays within your angelic body as a memory. This leads to lack of self-esteem, low confidence and depression and may either cause you to rebel as a defence mechanism or drive you to change your ways in order to conform with society's expectations. Either way, you will not feel truly happy within yourself. Angels will cleanse all memories of your not having been accepted and the effect this cruel judgement has had upon you. Through Angel Healing, you gain confidence to stand your ground and eventually turn the situation around by getting others to see a different perspective on living according to your values, rather than theirs. Acceptance is the beginning of healing. Unless you can acknowledge that everything exists in the form it is in, nothing can be changed.

Change

After accepting your situation, the next step that needs to be taken before healing can begin is to have the intention to change, followed by dedication and focus in achieving that intention. It may take time for all the energies to integrate within your angelic body, and before you start seeing results. This is the test of your patience, trust and faith. If you need more of these pure energies, your Guardian Angel will bring them into your awareness in the highest and best way. Keeping a personal journal throughout your healing journey will show you how far you have come, and reading back over your Angel experiences will inspire you to inspire others to change.

ANGEL HEALING MEDITATION FOR CLEANSING

ANGEL SECRET:

'Peace arrives when you piece your soul back together.'

CROWN CHAKRA

Angel Starlight enters your angelic body through a beautiful white rose just above your physical body. You see a silvery

sparkling star in the centre of your crown chakra and connect with your soul. Your Guardian Angel shows you the areas of your soul which need cleansing as dark spots within the star.

THIRD-EYE CHAKRA

Angel Starlight travels down into the purple rose between your two eyes and into your mind. It now begins to clear your intuition blocks. Your Guardian Angel takes you on a journey back into your past to remember when or where parts of your soul became detached from you. You will now remember traumatic and very tearful times when you lost particles of your soul.

THROAT CHAKRA

Angel Starlight travels down into the blue rose in your throat and extends towards your ears. Your Guardian Angel now prays that all soul particles belonging to you be cleansed with the Angel Starlight and returned to you now. In your mind's eye, visualize that you are taken to Archangel Raphael's healing sanctuary and that you are lying on a white bed. As you relax even more, you start seeing tiny silvery sparkling stars coming into your face and running up to your crown chakra, reconnecting with your soul.

HEART CHAKRA

Angel Starlight travels down into the green rose within your heart and, as it blossoms, you see that it slowly transforms into a pink rose. Your Guardian Angel now shows you who your soul particles were left with. Were they lost because of a relationship breakdown, or through grieving? As you travel deeper into your heart, notice any negative cords that may still be binding you together with this person and see that the Angel Starlight now shines upon the cords, dissolving them. As soon as all negative cords are removed, you begin to feel the pink unconditional love flowing from the core of your heart chakra all around your body.

SOLAR PLEXUS CHAKRA

Angel Starlight travels down into the yellow rose within your stomach area, the core of your being. Your Guardian Angel now helps you to find your golden core of inner power. You are now becoming stronger and more powerful as your soul begins to feel whole and complete. Any feelings of nausea or any other symptoms are now being healed by the Angel Starlight.

SACRAL CHAKRA

Angel Starlight travels down into the orange rose just below your navel and activates your creative abilities. Your Guardian Angel now asks you to look for the soul particles of others which you have been hanging on to. As soon as these are found, visualize the golden Angel Starlight energy cleansing them until they become completely pure again. Your Guardian Angel now calls upon the soul to whom these particles belong and arranges to hand them over. You now feel a sense of freedom as though heaviness has been lifted from you.

ROOT CHAKRA

Angel Starlight travels down into the red rose at the base of your spine. Your Guardian Angel will now completely lock in your soul particles to make you feel whole again. Visualize that you are now strengthening the connection between your body, mind, heart and soul. Your Guardian Angel places a shield of golden light around your entire angelic body to keep it safe, secure and pro-tected from any trauma to your soul in the future.

Success Story

Matt came for an Angel Reading because he felt he wasn't able to move forward in his life. When I linked into his energy, I was guided by the Angels to describe a certain place to him. I saw a young boy on a very busy road, and he seemed to be lost. He had been there for many years and wasn't ready to move on. When I explained to Matt what I had seen, initially, this made no sense to him. As he relaxed further, I took him on a journey through his subconscious mind so that he could understand what the Angels were trying to show him. We discovered that the little boy on the road was Matt, and he remembered that he had been involved in a car accident as a child. As this was a very traumatic experience, through fear, he had lost consciousness, and the Angels explained that he had also lost some particles of his soul. In the meditation, Matt was guided to rescue the little boy and bring him back. Afterwards, Matt told me that he had been feeling lost in his life for a very long time, and he now understood why he felt unable to move forward. He began confidently making major life-changing decisions soon after his session and was so amazed at the power of the mind that he went on to study and qualify as a hypnotherapist.

Negative Energy

Ill-wishing

'Psychic attack' is the term used when there is an ill-wishing towards you that comes from another person. This attack can occur on a conscious or subconscious level, which means that the person doesn't necessarily have to have the intention of directing this attack at you. They may be expressing their anger by speaking out negative words about you, and these thought forms will be picked up by your soul. Your Guardian Angel will protect you in every way when you ask for assistance. Sometimes hidden blessings come from psychic attacks, though often after a great deal of misery, but it is for this reason that the Angels are not able to stop them happening. For example, if you experience loss or depression because of ill-wishing, this may open your mind to spiritual healing or push you to go for counselling, which will be very beneficial for you in many ways. Every thought holds an energetic frequency, and the emotion behind the thought drives this thought to become an action.

Negative Cords

The Angels are able to cut the invisible negative energetic cords binding you to previous partners, holding you in a negative place and stopping you from moving forward. Although you may have physically moved away from the past, you may have some emotional, mental or spiritual attachments which are still holding you in the past. Emotions of regret, guilt or anger flow between these cords and, subsequently, they have a negative impact or attack on your peace. These negative cords are usually attached between chakras, for example between two solar plexuses if there are constant power struggles, or between two sacral chakras if there is an unhealthy sexual attachment. Negative cords look like dark and thick ropes or tubes. Bitter feelings and thoughts pass through them as if going through a tunnel. When they are cut, it brings a sense of freedom and release. Cords are formed and attached to people you interact with on a daily basis, therefore cleansing meditations are very helpful and useful, especially for all-round well-being. After arguments, visualize your Guardian Angel cutting the cords between you and showering you with the golden Angel Starlight. You will immediately feel much better and will have no room in your heart to hold grudges.

Positive Cords

Soul mates have very strong cords between them, attached between the crown chakras. They look like a beautiful rainbow. Unconditional love and healing light constantly flows through these cords, even before you meet each other physically. These positive cords cannot ever be cut by the Angels, as you belong to the same soul family. As soul-mate relationships are very challenging, unfortunately negative cords are created because of the frustration, sadness and anger you experience before learning a soul lesson. On one hand, you are receiving pure love, however, on the other hand, you may also be receiving what your conscious mind perceives as hate. This is why, after separating from a soul mate, you will endure an inner battle of love and hate until you cut the negative cords, stop the bad feelings and learn to cope with, understand and manage the feeling of love without needing to be in a relationship again.

Surrender

The Angels help you to let go of the negativity by asking you to surrender the problem or person to them. They will deal with the situation with love and without judgement and they are happy to take the burden from your shoulders. Miraculously, you will no longer be expecting that telephone call or have any other expectations that the other person will make you happy. Angels will help you to feel emotionally balanced, and also independent. What tends to happen in relationships that have been through a rough patch is that, as soon as you set the intention of letting go and cutting negative cords, healing energy flows in and purifies the relationship and brings clarity to both parties. Once this happens, the partners in the relationship are either reconciled in an unexpected way, or you realize that the relationship has fulfilled this purpose and you naturally move on with your life.

ANGEL HEALING MEDITATION FOR NEGATIVE ENERGY

ANGEL SECRET:

'Negative perception is only deception, innocence is your benevolence.'

CROWN CHAKRA

Angel Starlight enters your angelic body through a beautiful white rose just above your physical body. You see a silvery sparkling star in the centre of your crown chakra and connect with your soul. Your Guardian Angel expands and cleanses your soul as it prepares for healing negative energy around your angelic body.

THIRD-EYE CHAKRA

Angel Starlight travels down into the purple rose between your two eyes and into your mind. It now begins to clear your intuition blocks. Your Guardian Angel shows you your beautiful inner eye opening. Scan your entire angelic body now to find the dark negative cords and ask your Guardian Angel to pull them out of both of your chakras. Angel Starlight is being poured into your angelic body and purifying the areas where cords have been pulled out. The conflict is now completely healed between you and the people involved, and this will show very soon in your emotions, thoughts and actions.

THROAT CHAKRA

Angel Starlight travels down into the blue rose in your throat and extends towards your ears. Your Guardian Angel now helps you to visualize any spirit attachments that may be trying to get your attention. You now ask them to leave and go towards the light for their own development. Call Archangel Michael if you feel fearful about doing this. Visualize that your whole body becomes a golden bright light which is protecting you from lower energies. Once you know that they have been released from around you, visualize a shower of golden Angel Starlight coming down like a waterfall and washing over your whole angelic body and the room you are in.

HEART CHAKRA

Angel Starlight travels down into the green rose within your heart and, as it blossoms, you see that it slowly transforms into a pink rose. Your Guardian Angel now gives you the energy of compassion. As you become more aware of this energy, begin to direct it towards anyone who may have directly or indirectly wished ill thoughts towards you, through their anger, insecurities or jealousy. Angels now open your heart even more with compassion so that you can understand why other people behave the way they do. They also remind you that love is the greatest healer.

SOLAR PLEXUS CHAKRA

Angel Starlight travels down into the yellow rose within your stomach area, the core of your being. Your Guardian Angel now reconnects you with your inner power. See that Angel Starlight is now directly beaming down into this area, washing away the fear or loss of control within you that was caused by these negative attachments. As your inner power comes forward, you let go of all desires for revenge and release them to the Angels.

SACRAL CHAKRA

Angel Starlight travels down into the orange rose just below your navel and activates your creative abilities. Your Guardian Angel asks you to review your own actions towards others. If you have labelled yourself as a victim, then it's time to transmute that label into victory with the Angel Starlight. You are being completely cleansed now, and the Angels are reconnecting you to your true essence. Feel that you are now ready to live as an Angel, therefore seeing everything through Angel eyes, and feeling with Angel heart, which knows only love.

ROOT CHAKRA

Angel Starlight travels down into the red rose at the base of your spine. Your Guardian Angel gives you the feeling and knowledge that you are free from all attachments to past relationships or situations. You feel brighter, happier and no longer feel a heaviness pulling you down. You are constantly channelling the Angel Starlight, and your soul is shining a very bright and beautiful light through you which immediately dissipates negative energy.

Success Story

Faye sought Angel Healing to try to stop the psychic attack she felt was being directed at her by her in-laws. From the start of her relationship with her husband, she noticed that certain of her husband's family members were constantly interfering and causing trouble because they were jealous. As it was not in Faye's nature to be confrontational, she continued to be nice to them, even though, every time she was around them, she would end up feeling physically ill, emotionally drained and full of negative thoughts about herself and her marriage. During her meditation, we invoked Archangel Michael to cut away at the negative cords between her and her husband's family. Physically, Faye started to feel a pulling sensation, especially in her back. The Angels showed me that all psychic attacks, such as energetic daggers, enter our energetic bodies from the back – the feeling is very much like that of being stabbed in the back. This was a very emotional releasing exercise for Faye, and she cried throughout the meditation. She felt like a victim and didn't understand why she was being attacked by these people's negative thoughts and ill wishes. Once Archangel Michael had cut the cords, he showed me that all traces of negativity in her body, mind, heart and soul were being transmuted by the healing light. In addition, she was given a protection exercise to carry out every day, especially when she felt negative energy around her. The Angels then guided Faye to communicate with the souls of her attackers and find out what their motive was. It turned out that her mother-in-law no longer felt loved by her son, and her sister-in-law was in an unhappy marriage and jealous of Faye's happiness. Together, we directed healing energy to both of these women and, within a few weeks, Faye's relationship with them had miraculously healed.

Attracting Soul Mates

Strong Connections

At some stage of your life, you may feel a very strong connection to someone and find that a relationship with this person is very challenging but that you are unable to walk away from it. Usually, these difficult relationships are the ones you learn and grow from the most, and it's these people who play a hugely important role in your spiritual development. Angels help soul mates to communicate and link together on a different level while you are asleep or during meditations. Together with your soul mate, you will discuss what your needs are and how you can help each other at that point in your life. Sometimes, before incarnating, it is pre-arranged when, how and why we will meet on Earth. However, through free will, these arrangements can be altered, delayed and even cancelled. While you are awake, your soul will speak to you through your intuition or through your Angels, telling you where to go, at what time and how to recognize your soul mate. This is why, when you actually meet, there is a sense of having known this person 'all your life' within a very short space of time. Your souls will remember each other very clearly, and they even know the purpose of meeting up at this time, however the conscious mind cannot make any sense of it or rationalize it.

Angelic Love

Once you have begun your spiritual development, you naturally become more open to angelic and soul love. Whether you can allow yourself to receive this love or not depends on whether you love yourself enough to say you really do deserve it and that you are worthy of being loved. When you value yourself enough, receiving love from your Angels and soul mates becomes a part of your everyday life. When you experience angelic love it feels as if your heart is overflowing with all the goodness and blessings you could ever wish for. There is a sense of such overwhelming contentment and gratitude for every single thing and person in your life, and nothing else really matters. Having these emotions on a regular basis will make you stand out from a crowd of people who are too afraid to open up and show love, whatever their reasons may be. Your role is to send out the vibrations of love, and these will penetrate their angelic bodies and filter through them, even if they are not consciously aware of this happening. It will also attract much love into your own life in all forms, and especially very special soul mates, who will want to share love with you.

Peace

Your logical mind will become stressed by over-thinking and analysing why you may not have a soul mate in your life right now, and this will bring you down emotionally. Take time out in your Angels' Sanctuary and call upon your Guardian Angel to answer the following questions for you. What do I need to change within myself in order to attract my soul mate? How am I blocking this relationship? What are my fears about loving someone very deeply? What do I want from a soul-mate relationship? When you quieten the conscious mind, you will be able to receive clear guidance as well as healing energy to help you to heal your heart from past hurtful situations. When you have connected with your own soul, Angels will help you to attract your soul mate into your life to help you feel love in the highest and best way possible.

Perfect Life Partner

You may be wishing to bring into your life the most perfect life partner, however this may not be the right time for you to settle down. There could be so much more that you need to learn about, either independently or through relationships with others, which will make you completely whole and happy so that you won't have unreasonable expectations from your life partner. Your Guardian Angel knows what your future holds. When you become intuitive and listen carefully to the inner guidance of your soul and of your Angels, they will bring you opportunities to complete everything you need to do before guiding you to find your life partner.

Soul Connection

Before you meet in the physical world, you can make contact with your soul mate on a soul level. During a meditation, you can travel into a higher realm, such as the spiritual realm, and call upon a soul mate to connect with you. As you have many soul mates, they will all appear in your life at the appropriate moment, in the correct order of your life experiences and to teach you what you need to learn at that moment. However, you may connect with a soul mate on a soul level now, and they may physically come into your life many years later – or perhaps not in this but in another lifetime. Behind the scenes, Guardian Angels link with the Guardian Angels of the souls that will be coming into your life, in order to devise an action plan for you both to meet in the physical world. They will whisper guidance into your ears so that you can magically be in the right place at the right time together. Your soul will instantly recognize the person when your eyes meet in the physical realm. You have a very large soul family, who are different from your family in this world. These soul family members will come into your life at any point as soul mates to be part of your life. Although many people believe that soul mates are only ever relationship partners, they can also be family members, for example, your children; or even your friends. When you eventually meet your soul mate in the physical world, Angels sing and dance around you as you experience love in the purest form through your reunion.

ANGEL HEALING MEDITATION TO ATTRACT SOUL MATES

ANGEL SECRET:

'Find your soul mate with your heart; love their heart with your soul.'

CROWN CHAKRA

Angel Starlight enters your angelic body through a beautiful white rose just above your physical body. You see a silvery sparkling star in the centre of your crown chakra and connect with your soul. As it grows and expands, it covers the whole of your body. Within a few seconds, you see that this soul now looks like an Angel, and it steps out of your body, ready to go on a journey to meet your soul mate.

THIRD-EYE CHAKRA

Angel Starlight travels down into the purple rose between your two eyes and into your mind. It now begins to clear your intuition blocks. Visualize and feel your soul start flying higher and higher, away from the Earth, passing the universe, until you get to the angelic realm. There you meet your Guardian Angel, who is waiting for you.

THROAT CHAKRA

Angel Starlight travels down into the blue rose in your throat and extends towards your ears. Your Guardian Angel now guides you to the spiritual realm, where your soul lives with your soul family in between incarnations on Earth. You meet many soul family members who have been waiting to greet you. You are now being guided into a special room where you will meet your soul mate. Your Guardian Angel leaves you here.

HEART CHAKRA

Angel Starlight travels down into the green rose within your heart and, as it blossoms, you see that it slowly transforms into a pink rose. Connect with your heartbeat as you feel more and more excited. From a distance, you see a shining star coming your way. As it comes closer, your heart beats faster and you now see a beautiful pink cord extending from the centre of your heart chakra, reaching out to attract and attach itself to this soul.

SOLAR PLEXUS CHAKRA

Angel Starlight travels down into the yellow rose within your stomach area, the core of your being. As your soul mate comes closer towards you, you start to feel an overwhelming sense of happiness, recognizing this as a soul reunion which you have longed for. This soul will play a very important role in your life and will teach you many lessons in order for you to grow and fulfil your soul purpose.

SACRAL CHAKRA

Angel Starlight travels down into the orange rose just below your navel and activates your creative abilities. As the two stars unite and merge into one, see that both of your golden angelic bodies are intertwined together, sharing spiritual love. This is a beautiful, sacred union of your souls, and you look forward to sharing many beautiful moments together in the physical world, as you are in the angelic world.

ROOT CHAKRA

Angel Starlight travels down into the red rose at the base of your spine. Your soul mate will appear when you are ready for them physically and will stay until they have completed their mission. Time is not relevant in the spiritual realm, as a few moments can seem like years ,and days can seem like lifetimes. Everything will come into your physical life in perfect timing in accordance with your life plan. Thank your soul mate for connecting with you and tell them that you look forward to meeting them in the physical world. Send love to all your soul family members before you leave, to come back down into your body, fully grounding your-self and bringing your awareness to your breath.

Success Story

For many years, I dreamt of a sacred reunion with a very special soul. Although I could never see his physical form, I remember looking into blue, sparkling and mesmerizing eyes. By learning to channel my Guardian Angel, I started to receive written guidance about this soul and how we would meet. Without going into details, the meeting with this blue-eyed man did take place, and we both felt an almost other-worldly connection. It took me a long time to come to terms with the fact that our relationship was not meant to be that of life-long partners. After a great deal of heartbreak and soul-searching, I realized that this man had come into my life to show me my true path, and that my life purpose was to commit myself to spreading Angel Healing and love. Over the years, I had transferred all the information channelled to me into my diaries and, looking back on it, I understood that, at the time, I was blinded by my need and misinterpreted the Angels' messages. Now, I can see that everything they told me was true, and that my Angels were protecting me and preparing me for my true life journey.

Meeting Your Soul Family

Spiritual Realm

There are many different realms, also known as planes or king-doms, that humans are connected to but have not fully explored or embraced. The Angels live in a place of pure love which has no duality called the angelic realm. The spiritual realm is the home of all souls who are on a sacred journey of evolving and developing. In the spiritual realm, there are many different levels and places that the soul will travel through, before and after rein-carnating into the Earth realm. Angels are not required to guide the souls in the spiritual realm as much as they are needed in the Earth realm.

Spirit Guides

Your main spirit guide will stay with you from birth and help you through your soul awakening, until you connect with your angelic self and no longer require their guidance. They will move on to fulfilling their own missions in the spiritual realm once they know that you are okay. Throughout your life, your Guardian Angel will regularly meet with your spirit guides to discuss your healing needs and how they will work together to help you along your journey. Your main spirit guide has the very big responsibility of keeping you on your spiritual path, even when the transition periods are very difficult for you. Although they have much compassion for you and will send you healing and strength, they are unable to stop the challenges from coming into your life, as this will interfere with your learning. You have free will as to whether you wish to follow your life path or not. If you choose not to, on a very deep soul level, you will feel unfulfilled, as that is the reason for coming to Earth.

Soul Family

Each person has a soul family in the spiritual realm which consists of many different spirit guides who will come into your life and provide guidance through certain phases, such as education, career, relationships, etc. Before you began your life on Earth, you made an agreement with all of the members in your soul family about the roles that will be played by each one. Some of these soul family members will remain in the spiritual realm and play a role in guiding you on a soul level, and others will reincarnate into a life on Earth at the same time as you. They will play a role in your life as either a family member related by blood or as a soul mate, either in form of a relationship or a very close friend. They will all help you along your journey by fulfilling their responsibility as agreed in the spiritual realm before your life began. This is why soul mates teach us the hardest lessons, but they do us the biggest favours and, on a soul level, it is easier to forgive them.

Relatives in Spirit

When your family members on Earth pass away, they go back to the spiritual realm. If they suffered trauma in their lives through illness or depression, they will go to a healing sanctuary in the spiritual realm in order to recover. Angels are able to help you to develop your intuition and channelling skills so that you can make contact with your relatives in spirit. It is important to honour and respect your relatives' soul journey and free will and whether or not they are willing or able to communicate with you. What you can be sure of is that when your relative in spirit has been through their healing journey and has accepted that they are no longer in a body, they will somehow bring you a message of love through many signs that will help you remember them.

Children in Spirit

Angels understand your pain at losing a soul family member who chose to come into your life as your child. Miscarriages or abortions are very traumatic to the mother, even if they do not actually see the soul in a human body, because of the soul connection that existed between them on a higher level. Angels want you to know that the souls of children who may have been lost never hold any grudges towards the mother or any other member of the family. They are grateful and appreciate their journey from the spiritual realm into the womb, for however long it lasted. Angels look after the souls of children, ensuring that they find their way back to the light and are able to reunite with other soul members in the spiritual realm. When they are ready, these souls will become active spirit guides, looking after and guiding the parents through their trauma of bereavement or loss. Angels say that sometimes these children actually grow in the spirit world as though they would have in the Earth realm, or they will incarnate at the mother's next pregnancy. Either way, they are never actually lost or disconnected from the family.

ANGEL HEALING MEDITATION TO MEET YOUR SOUL FAMILY

ANGEL SECRET:

'Soul relatives teach you about relating to your soul.'

CROWN CHAKRA

Angel Starlight enters your angelic body through a beautiful white rose just above your physical body. You see a silvery sparkling star in the centre of your crown chakra and connect with your soul. Your soul now leaves your physical body and goes on a journey to the spiritual realm. Visualize that a strong silver cord is attached to the chakra so your soul will eventually comes back to connect with your angelic body.

THIRD-EYE CHAKRA

Angel Starlight travels down into the purple rose between your two eyes and into your mind. It now begins to clear any blocks on your intuition. See that you are now flying higher, passing the Earth and the universe until you come to a beautiful golden sky. As you float higher, you enter the spiritual realm through two very large golden doors with a golden Angel standing on each side. They welcome you and guide you to your soul family. You climb many golden steps to ascend into the higher levels of the spiritual realm. You are floating higher, with the Angels by your side. You come to another set of golden doors which are a bit smaller. As you walk through, you are greeted by a group of souls who are your soul family.

THROAT CHAKRA

Angel Starlight travels down into the blue rose in your throat and extends towards your ears. You now embrace your soul family and join the celebration and rituals they are having in honour of your reunion. You may or may not recognize these souls, but you feel very much at home. You settle into the group before a very special soul comes to join you. First of all, you see that your Guardian Angel has now appeared in the middle of your group and is shining the golden Angel Starlight energy into your soul and angelic body in order to raise your energetic frequency. As this happens, you now begin to communicate with your soul family in the language of love.

HEART CHAKRA

Angel Starlight travels down into the green rose within your heart and, as it blossoms, you see that it slowly transforms into a pink rose. Your Guardian Angel now brings your awareness to your heartbeat within your physical body. Even though your consciousness is up in the spiritual realm, you are still aware of your physical body too. Your heart begins to feel the excitement of meeting your spirit guide. Your soul family members begin a special ritual to prepare for this moment. Listen with your heart to the music, singing or chanting of your soul family and feel yourself joining in.

SOLAR PLEXUS CHAKRA

Angel Starlight travels down into the yellow rose within your stomach area, the core of your being. Visualize beautiful golden beams of light shining within the whole room that you are in. Another set of doors opens up in a distance quite high above you, and you see a beautiful golden goddess standing at the door. This soul is my spirit guide Ptara, and she is here to bring forward your spirit guide. You see that another soul joins Ptara and notice if the soul represents feminine or masculine essence. Your spirit guide floats downwards to join you and your soul family as Ptara closes the golden doors and disappears. As you reunite with your spirit guide, you both take a seat upon two golden thrones and begin to communicate about your soul's journey and life on Earth.

SACRAL CHAKRA

Angel Starlight travels down into the orange rose just below your navel and activates your creative abilities. Ask your spirit guide about your children in spirit. Whatever your situation on Earth is regarding having children, your spirit guide will now tell you how many children you have in the spirit realm, either waiting to come to Earth, or connected to you from the spiritual realm. You take this opportunity to speak with the souls of your children as your spirit guide brings them forward. Visualize and feel yourself embracing and sharing the strong loving feeling between you.

ROOT CHAKRA

Angel Starlight travels down into the red rose at the base of your spine. Your Guardian Angel will now prepare to come back into your physical body. Before you leave, you see and feel yourself saying goodbye to your spirit guide and soul family for now, as you embrace them all, one by one. Your Guardian Angel now guides you out towards the golden doors, which are being guarded by the two Angels who guided you in earlier. As you go through these doors, you start descending the golden steps until you get to the main large golden doors which are the entrance into the spiritual realm. The two Angels now say goodbye to you as you and your Guardian Angel float down through the golden sky, all the way down through the universe, towards the Earth realm and back into your physical body. Bringing your awareness to your whole body and, taking a few deep breaths in, slowly open your eyes and come back into the room.

Success Story

In 2007, I had the opportunity to go to Egypt, and there something extraordinary happened. Visiting the Pyramids was a very sacred experience and took me back to my spiritual roots. I felt excited but apprehensive before I entered the Great Pyramid. As soon as I stepped in, I felt very emotional, as if I was experiencing a past life memory, so I asked the Angels to help calm me down. Afterwards, at the hotel, I was mentally and physically exhausted, and spiritually restless. I decided to do some Angel Healing and fell into a deep meditation. My Guardian Angel took me back to my past life in Egypt and showed me the spiritual connection I had to it. In my meditation, I went back to my past life, initially by regressing to my birth, then I came into a very long corridor with lots of golden doors, which represented all my past lives. I came to one of the furthest doors, one of my earlier soul reincarnations. As I walked through the golden doors with my Guardian Angel's guidance, I entered a beautiful temple and saw in front of me a group of women I recognized. They were sitting in a circle, all dressed in white robes, and I knew that they were my soul sisters and healers. They welcomed me in, and I felt a very special reunion with them. We climbed higher, up some golden steps, until I stood in front of a throne upon which sat a beautiful Egyptian goddess. She held out her arms, and I knelt in front of her. She held me, and we both felt very happy to see each other again. She wanted to take me back to my memories of our lifetime together.

She explained that, once upon a time, there was a young girl who suffered emotional trauma until the age of eighteen. She had been abused and abandoned by her family for disobeying their wishes of her marrying a wealthy man of their choice. Her father was a powerful emperor, but his business had failed and his land had been taken from him, leaving many former dependents homeless and without income. Her mother had passed away when she was young and she missed her terribly, however she had managed to find a long-lost auntie.

I was told by my Guardian Angel that I was the girl and my spirit guide now was this auntie. She had adopted me and allowed me into her small circle of working women who performed healing for others. I was shown that I had died an old woman and had dedicated my life to healing others. Although I had never married or had my own children, I was happy and content because I knew I had fulfilled my life purpose. Through this meditation, I was able to relate the story of my past life to my current life purpose.

Living as an Earth Angel

Angelic Actions

To practise living as an Earth Angel means to live as your soul. The true essence of your soul is innocent, wise and pure, and these qualities should be reflected in your actions. Each step you take should take into account the feelings of other people, as well as the consequences it will have on Earth. As each person takes responsibility for their actions, the world will become a better place, with people reuniting and connecting with each other's true essence rather than through their egos. Choose your reactions towards others' actions and learn how to teach them a better way of thinking, feeling and behaving.

Angel Charity Work

Choose to be part of a charity organization and know that, however small or large your role is, you will still have a part to play in helping people who are in need. This is a beautiful way of giving unconditional love, through sacrificing some of your precious time to make a change in another's life. Your reward will be from the angelic realm and may come in any form that they feel is most relevant for you at that point in your life. When you give unconditionally, you open opportunities to receive from the universe.

Angelic Environment

Living your life in a harmonious and peaceful environment will have a major influence on your well-being and happiness. If you feel that it's time to freshen up your home or workplace, the Angels will feel a lot more attracted to your environments and therefore be around you a lot more. Burning incense, candles and having wind chimes constantly purifies your space and will draw many people into your home or workplace. Flowers, crystals and Angel figurines are also very uplifting and will change your energy. It is important to have environmental awareness and get into a good habit of recycling.

Angel Gifts

One of the biggest gifts that you can give back to the Angels is to spread their love to other people. As an Earth Angel, you may feel called to teach, heal or read for others. This is a beautiful gift for both the Angels and the people you are helping. Wherever possible, buy gifts of Angel books, figurines, posters or any other items representing the Angels for those who you love. These items will trigger love and peace in the person's life, which will create hope, health and happiness. A simple kind gesture such as a smile, helping someone, taking time to ask how they are, will mean so much to them, as it shows that you take an interest and will lift their spirits high. These gestures are priceless, yet so precious.

Angel Journal

Monitor your healing journey and life as an Earth Angel by keeping an Angel journal. Record your channelled messages so that you can look back and read them for inspiration in the future. Your life will be filled with ups and downs, however, when you see things from an Angel's perspective, suddenly the problem you are faced with doesn't seem so difficult to deal with. Be kind to yourself by releasing your thoughts and emotions regularly before they build up and cause havoc within you. Keep your inner world as organized as your outer world and spend your quality time enjoying life and planning something beneficial to you rather than dwelling on unnecessary issues.

Angel Meetings

Hold small meetings to spend time discussing Angel stories, doing Angel Healing meditations and giving others Angel messages through channelling. This makes a wonderful social gathering and will bring like-minded people together. Angel meetings create a very large amount of beautiful healing energy which can then be directed to a place in the world where it is needed most. As an Earth Angel, be an inspirational example and encourage those who are early on in their healing journey not to give up. Share insights of your transformational story, what your plans for the future are and how you plan on achieving them. Inspiring people is a very uplifting gift of hope and faith.

Angel Prayers

As an Earth Angel never forget each step of your journey and show gratitude at every moment in your life. By honouring the Angels for how much they have helped you to achieve the life you have now through prayers, you form a very special and sacred union with the angelic realm. Prayers should be said not only when you are in need, but also in gratitude for all that you have.

An act of unconditional love is when you pray for someone else's well-being or achievement on their behalf, even if they are not aware that you are doing so.

ANGEL HEALING MEDITATION FOR LIVING AS AN EARTH ANGEL

ANGEL SECRET:

'Earth Angels carry love from Angels to Earth and fear from Earth to Angels.'

CROWN CHAKRA

Angel Starlight enters your angelic body through a beautiful white rose just above your physical body. You see a silvery sparkling star in the centre of your crown chakra and connect with your soul. Visualize that it is shining very bright and is becoming larger until it grows to the size of your physical body. Feel the sparkles of your soul penetrating through your whole angelic body and expanding and cleansing all levels of your being. Feel that the energy of your soul is now going through into your cells, organs and bloodstream.

THIRD-EYE CHAKRA

Angel Starlight travels down into the purple rose between your two eyes and into your mind. It now begins to clear any blocks on your intuition. Visualize your whole physical body and all layers of your angelic body beaming with sparkling silvery white light. In a few moments, this energy will start turning into gold and you will see your angelic self emerge and step out of your body. Visualize yourself now standing over your body and directing Angel Starlight into your physical body, just as your Guardian Angel does when you need healing.

THROAT CHAKRA

Angel Starlight travels down into the blue rose in your throat and extends towards your ears. Your Guardian Angel now appears beside your angelic self. You are still glowing with white and golden light, with Angel Starlight energy emanating through your energetic hands. Your Guardian Angel now tells you about your Earth Angel healing responsibilities and you discuss who in your life, or in another place in the world, needs Angel Healing and how you can help. Visualize that you have energetic Angel wings which are extending from your back and slowly growing. See that you and your Guardian Angel now travel to be in the place energetically. As you travel, you are aware of the silver cord that attaches your soul to your physical body and will always pull you back there when your mission is complete.

HEART CHAKRA

Angel Starlight travels down into the green rose within your heart and, as it blossoms, you see that it slowly transforms into a pink rose. Your Guardian Angel now guides you back to stand beside your physical body. Bring your awareness to your heart on all levels of your angelic body. The Angel Starlight energy is now swirling through your heart chakra, transmuting the green into pink, and then into a beautiful gold rose. From this moment onwards, your heart will function with unconditional love as an Angel, in every situation you are faced with, in all areas of your life and most especially in your relationships.

SOLAR PLEXUS CHAKRA

Angel Starlight travels down into the yellow rose within your stomach area, the core of your being. You see that Archangel

Gabriel now descends to stand by your side. You notice that this Archangel is very much taller than your angelic self and see that he is filling you with a very bright yellow and golden energy of angelic wisdom and intelligence. You now know your soul purpose very clearly and feel ready to follow it by working alongside the Archangels to help humanity towards complete happiness through healing.

SACRAL CHAKRA

Angel Starlight travels down into the orange rose just below your navel and activates your creative abilities. You see that Archangel Chamuel now descends to stand by your side. He is now activating your deep, inner creative knowledge and talents in order to bring healing to those who are having relationship problems and challenges. Chamuel is now also activating your empathetic qualities so that you will become a natural intuitive and emanate the Angel Starlight unconsciously to all those who need it.

ROOT CHAKRA

Angel Starlight travels down into the red rose at the base of your spine. You see that Archangel Michael now descends to be by your side. He is now giving you the responsibilities which, as an Earth Angel, you will be carrying out. Archangel Michael is one of the Archangels who became the Guardian Angel of all Earth Angels, also known as light workers. He works very closely with Archangel Metatron, who is the Guardian Angel of all spiritual children who are being born into the Earth now. They are the future masters, as they are highly wise and intelligent souls. Now that you are an Earth Angel, repeat the affirmation: 'I am blessed to work alongside the beautiful Angels to bring love and light to Earth.'

Success Story

Sonia had Angel Healing in order to enhance her connection with the Angelic Realm. During her meditation, I was shown that she was carrying a beautiful beam of white light within her aura and she was naturally glowing, which many people would pick up on. The Angels explained that Sonia had had a very tough childhood and had faced many challenges and feelings of not belonging in this world. Her mixed cultural background added to the pressures she experienced while growing up and trying to find her true identity. She had dedicated her life to a force beyond the earthly realms and believed that the spiritual path was the one she should follow in order to achieve understanding, inner peace and self-acceptance. Sonia resonated with the Angels' interpretation of her life in the past, and she felt ready to meet her Guardian Angel, who had protected her through all those years. This was a beautiful and very emotional experience for her, as it confirmed to her everything she was already feeling and hearing in her personal meditations and prayers. Sonia was told that she was indeed an Earth Angel and had already changed many people's lives, both directly and indirectly, as they came into contact with her. She has attracted many influential people into her life from all over the world and is following her Guardian Angel's advice in order to spread love and healing across the world through her creative and angelic gifts.

Practical Exercises with Archangel Michael
(Channelling Wisdom for Healing the Soul)

Awakening Your Soul

Each person has many roles to play throughout the journey of their life. These roles and the many masks that you wear will shape your personality and determine your identity. Close your eyes and see the many roles you have, such as parent, sibling, spouse, profes- sional, friend, etc. Ask yourself, who am I really when all these roles have been taken away? Identify with your true essence, your soul. Take the focus off your external world and keep looking deeply within until you see the darkness slowly fading away as a beautiful bright white or colourful light emerges. Connect with qualities that your soul represents, such as peace, wisdom and oneness, rather than with separation. Start to live your everyday life using these qualities at every opportunity.

Intuition

Each day at every opportunity, allow yourself to exercise your natural intuitive and healing abilities to enhance happiness and well-being in your life and in others' lives. Practise using your intuitive skills by link- ing into your future before living it; for example, at the beginning of each day, write down your premonitions of who you may unexpect-edly come into contact with or what you may experience. Practise using your healing skills by linking into another person's angelic body, with their permission, to scan their physical, mental, emotional and spiritual bodies for information regarding their well-being. Relay the information you pick up by channelling your intuition through your third-eye and throat chakras, and direct healing energy where required through your crown and hand chakras.

Cleansing

Learn how to switch off from the external chaos, loudness and distractions by practising the art of cleansing your inner and outer world regularly. True inner peace and serenity comes from within, and is mastered when you allow nothing and no one to take that feeling away from you. It is the most beautiful state of being you can maintain and feel empowered by. The Angels are constantly in a very peaceful place and can bestow this energy upon any area where there may be disruption. When you witness any form of upheaval, call upon me to cleanse the negativity and help you to detach from the situation. Ask the Angels to direct their healing energies to areas around your planet that are experiencing natural disasters or any upheaval.

Negative Energy

When you have been around someone who has completely drained you and you feel within your aura that you have picked up on negative energy, physically use your hands to sweep your energy field as though you are taking away the dark, heavy and dense energy and handing it to the Angels to take into the light. Then, using your hands, scan your entire body slowly, starting from the top of your head downwards and, as you come to each chakra, cut the negative cords that have been attached to your angelic body. See that the Angels cut the negative cords from the other end and take these energetic cords into the light too.

Attracting Soul Mates

In order to attract a soul mate, you need to be your own soul's mate! Take time out from using your body, mind and heart to dictate your life and practise communicating with your soul. Your soul is the Angel within you, the counterpart of your Guardian Angel and a component of your soul family. As your body, mind, heart and soul harmonize and link with your Guardian Angel, you will naturally and effortlessly be guided to start meeting your soul mates. When there is separation between your inner bodies and you are not acknowledging that you are part of oneness, there will be a sense of separation in your external world which leads to constantly searching for 'the one'.

Meeting Your Soul Family

To connect with your main spirit guide, get into a very relaxed and comfortable state by clearing your environment and doing a few deep-breathing exercises with your eyes closed. Play some soft music to raise the energetic frequencies of the room and, when you are ready, say out loud, 'My dear spirit guide, I invite you to channel your spiritual wisdom through me with regard to my situation … Thank you!' Ask a specific question – something you may be curious about or feel you need guidance on. Wait a few moments for the answer to come through you by way of verbal channelling. Your spirit guide will merge with your aura and speak through your throat chakra. Remain open to the answer, as it will come to you

at any time and in any form. There are many other ways this message can reach you, either intuitively shown to you through a
conversation with another person, or even through the lyrics of a
song that you will hear soon. Notice the signs!

Living as an Earth Angel

There is an Angel within each person. It takes an immense amount
of courage to live in your purest and open state, as you may feel
vulnerable to attack. Rest assured that when you open your heart
to love and invite the Angels close into your life, we will protect you
as if you are our beloved children. You deserve to live as your true
essence – your soul – without fear. In every moment of your existence and with every breath, have gratitude for all that you are – all
that you have and all that you are becoming. Work closely with the
angelic realm to banish the darkness upon Mother Earth and its
inhabitants. Allow us to shine the Angel Healing Energy and the
Angel Healing Secrets through you and many others as our gift to
humanity and our service to our beloved creator. Angel-ize each
situation you encounter by seeing it through Angel-eyes! Feel the
Angel's love in your heart and love like an Angel.

Acknowledgements

I would like to acknowledge and express my eternal love and gratitude to everyone who has played a part on the amazing journey that enabled me to write *The Secrets of Angel Healing*.

This book was channelled by my Guardian Angel, Exeline, who is a very beautiful being of light. I dedicate it to my precious family, most especially my mother, who awakened me to the angelic realm through her suffering. To my father, who I love dearly, and to whom I am forever thankful for his teachings, and also my two beautiful sisters Gamze and Bahar, who mean the world to me.

I wish to say a very special thank you and extend my deepest gratitude to my best friend Maximilian for supporting, encouraging and believing in me. Thank you for being by my side every step of the way and for teaching me about true unconditional love; this is a gift I will cherish forever.

I am blessed to have reunited with many of my soul mates in my lifetime. I send angelic love to my older Soul Sisters, Sonia Oscar, Selima Gurtler and Sibel Behzat. You have all been inspirational women who I admire and look up to for your incredible strength and wisdom. To my beautiful friend Lauren Greenwood-Davies, thank you for listening to me and being by my side through my difficulties.

To all the members of Purely Angels, my friends, clients and students, I thank you for trusting me and the Angels to help you on your healing journey. I love you all dearly. I also thank my teachers for helping me to grow spiritually and develop my intuition in order to fulfil my life's purpose.

And finally, most importantly I thank God and the angelic realm for the many blessings in my life and I ask for continuing divine guidance to awaken people to love and happiness through Angel Healing.